Unproduction Studies and the American Film Industry

This book makes the case for unproduction studies, the study of films left unmade, unseen, or unreleased, as a radical discipline with the potential to uncover a shadow history of the American film industry.

Exploring the archival methods that can be utilised in this endeavour, James Fenwick argues that a revisionist history is needed to understand the logic of the film industry, finding that it has long been predicated on a system of unmade creativity in which finances, resources, and labour are invested into projects that production companies know will never be produced or have no intention of ever producing. Using the Production Code Administration (PCA) records, housed at the Margaret Herrick Library, as a case study, the book explores the material existence of the unmade and considers how archives and archival methods can be used to construct a shadow history that recovers the forgotten, marginalised, and overlooked figures in film history, providing explanations for structural forces that contributed to the unmade.

Given its unique use of the unmade as an analytic for film history, this book will be an essential read for scholars interested in film and media history, performance studies, film production, and creative practice, as well as for archivists and archival researchers.

James Fenwick is a senior lecturer in the Department of Media Arts and Communication at Sheffield Hallam University, UK.

Routledge Focus on Film Studies

1 **Robot Ecology and the Science Fiction Film**
J. P. Telotte

2 **Weimar Cinema, Embodiment, and Historicity**
Cultural Memory and the Historical Films of Ernst Lubitsch
Mason Kamana Allred

3 **Migrants in Contemporary Spanish Film**
Clara Guillén Marín

4 **Virtue and Vice in Popular Film**
Joseph H. Kupfer

5 **Unproduction Studies and the American Film Industry**
James Fenwick

Unproduction Studies and the American Film Industry

James Fenwick

LONDON AND NEW YORK

First published 2022
by Routledge
2 Park Square, Milton Park, Abingdon, Oxon OX14 4RN

and by Routledge
605 Third Avenue, New York, NY 10158

Routledge is an imprint of the Taylor & Francis Group, an informa business

British Library Cataloguing-in-Publication Data
A catalogue record for this book is available from the British Library

Library of Congress Cataloging-in-Publication Data
Names: Fenwick, James (Film historian), author.
Title: Unproduction studies and the American film industry / James Fenwick.
Description: Abingdon, Oxon ; New York, NY : Routledge, 2022. | Series: Routledge focus on film studies | Includes bibliographical references and index.
Subjects: LCSH: Unfinished films—United States—History and criticism. | Motion picture industry—United States—History. | Motion pictures—History—Methodology.
Classification: LCC PN1993.5.U6 F43 2022 (print) | LCC PN1993.5.U6 (ebook) | DDC 791.430973—dc23
LC record available at https://lccn.loc.gov/2021019856
LC ebook record available at https://lccn.loc.gov/2021019857

ISBN: 9781032072210 (hbk)
ISBN: 9781032072487 (pbk)
ISBN: 9781003206118 (ebk)

DOI: 10.4324/9781003206118

Typeset in Times New Roman
by codeMantra

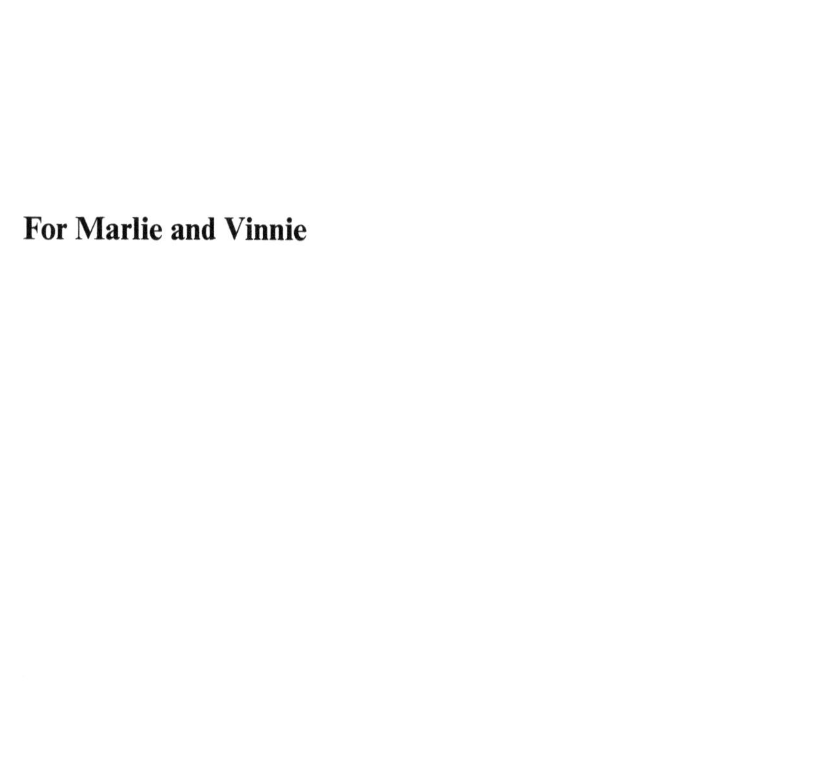

For Marlie and Vinnie

Contents

Tables

About the author

James Fenwick is a senior lecturer in the Department of Media Arts and Communication at Sheffield Hallam University. He is the author of *Stanley Kubrick Produces* (Rutgers University Press 2020), editor of *Understanding Kubrick's 2001: A Space Odyssey: Representations and Interpretations* (Intellect 2018), and co-editor with Kieran Foster and David Eldridge of *Shadow Cinema: The Historical and Production Contexts of Unmade Films* (Bloomsbury 2020). He is an editor of the *Open Screens* journal, series editor of *Unmade Film and Television* (Intellect), and co-convenor of the Archives and Archival Methods Special Interest Group (BAFTSS).

Preface

James Fenwick

My aim with this book is to offer an extended case study on the potential of unproduction studies, a field of enquiry that primarily uses archival research methods to uncover unmade, unseen, and unreleased film and television projects from across history. I do this via a case study of the Motion Picture Association of America Production Code Administration records (henceforth the PCA records) housed at the Margaret Herrick Library in Los Angeles. I had originally conceived the case study for an academic journal, but it soon became apparent that the study required a much more in-depth treatment than that allowed by the standard article length of 10,000 words given how unproduction studies is still an emerging subdiscipline within film and media studies. As such, the book commences with an extended reflection on the wider field before moving into a specific case study of the PCA records.

The case study in this book is focused on the unmade over the unseen and unreleased. It uses a sample of unmade films that are part of the PCA records. The aim is not to necessarily consider the history of the PCA—others have done this already—but rather to think about what the case study can tell us about the methods, approaches, and objectives of work in unproduction studies, with the PCA records serving as an investigation into the material potential of archival remnants of the unmade. The focus of the case study will be on those PCA records that are explicitly labelled as being unmade, or to use the terminology employed in the metadata of the Margaret Herrick Library's archival catalogue, 'unproduced'. Estimates suggest that there are between 1,000 and 2,000 individual film projects in the PCA records that are unproduced, out of approximately 20,000 film projects (Genevieve Maxwell, email message to author, June 9, 2020). In other words, around 10 percent of all projects in the PCA records are classed as unproduced. The case study looks at a sample of these unproduced records that are available digitally. The specific PCA records that I have consulted are listed in Appendix I.

I still feel a slight reticence in proclaiming myself a scholar of the unmade, not least because some filmmakers and screenwriters have confessed to fearing that their unmade work would be subjected to academic scrutiny. Take the novelist and experimental writer B. S. Johnson who, throughout his career, generated many ideas and projects that he submitted to film and television commissioning editors, most of which remained unmade. Johnson's greatest fear for his unmade and abandoned work was 'that "some academic c*nt will produce a study on it"' (Harle 2020). I also confess a reticence because, in many ways, the study of the unmade is a field that does not exist, from the fact there are no formal academic networks or associations to the problem that the primary objects of study remain conspicuously absent from known histories. Indeed, more often than not, there is nothing to study, bar a few scraps of paper—and that is if you are lucky.

Perhaps I should clarify how I came to be a scholar of the unmade. I began my academic career working with archives, using them in a bid to understand the material conditions of production of films that existed, that had received mainstream release in cinemas, and that were part of the canonical history of Hollywood. Two key archives that I worked with were the Stanley Kubrick Archive at the University of the Arts London and the Kirk Douglas Papers at the Wisconsin Center for Film and Theater Research. At each archive, I always had one intention in mind: to excavate as much data as possible on the films that had been produced in order to fully situate them within industrial contexts. Yet, each visit led to an increasing distraction when, perusing the catalogues, I would come across categories such as 'unproduced', 'unfinished', or 'potential projects'. These categories became an interesting aside that I would, if time permitted, look at with nothing more than fan-infused curiosity: the Stanley Kubrick filmography that might have been or the Kirk Douglas westerns that never were. But the fan curiosity soon evolved into a genuine scholarly interest, for it occurred to me that I was attempting to understand the material conditions of production of those films associated with Stanley Kubrick and Kirk Douglas, but there was an entire material resource that I was not using: the unmade, unseen, or unreleased projects. It was a scholarly interest further piqued by the way the unmade projects existed within the archive: usually it would be nothing more than a slim file containing a couple of notes, maybe a project title, or even just a cryptic letter with no contextualising detail. Hence my remark that the scholar of the unmade typically studies…nothing. As my research progressed, I soon realised that the unmade was not about filling the gaps of existing film history, but about exploring a shadow history that existed within the archives, an exploration of creativity, at times creative failure, and an investigation into the nature of what even constitutes the unmade.

The book proceeds as follows. Chapter 1 provides an extended overview of the current state of unproduction studies and works towards key definitions as well as the most appropriate methods and approaches being employed in the field at present. The chapter also emphasises the importance of the archive to unproduction studies and makes the case for the foregrounding of the materiality of the object of study: the unmade film project. This book is centred on archives and archival methods in a bid to highlight the absences and gaps in both the archives and in wider film and television history. Yet, rather than attempting to resolve these gaps and absences in material evidence and knowledge, the book makes the case for the construction of a counter history that celebrates these absences in a bid to accentuate the creative process, as well as the marginalised and the forgotten in film history. Chapters 2 to 7 then provide an in-depth case study of a particular archival collection: the unproduced category of the PCA records. Chapter 2 provides a brief contextual history of the production processes of the Hollywood studio system between the 1930s and 1950s, along with an overview of the PCA. Chapter 3 focuses on the PCA records and discusses their existence within the Margaret Herrick Library. The chapter also considers archival methods in more detail. Chapters 4 to 7 are case studies centred on the analysis of the records, focused on themes that are apparent within the archival documentation: women, sex, politics, and crime. These chapters investigate the material form of the unmade as well as the potential reasons for projects having been consigned to the unproduced category. The analysis focuses on structural barriers. It is apparent that there were often wider forces beyond the PCA that prevented projects from being produced. Taken together, the book explores the scholarly potential of unproduction studies, proposes aims and objectives for a wider scholarly endeavour, and considers the impact that the work in this area could have on the broader film and media studies community.

Works cited

Harle, Mattew. 2020. 'Not Enough Johnson.' *Sight & Sound* 31, no. 1: 24.

1 Unproduction studies

Unproduction studies is a burgeoning new field of enquiry. New in the sense that it remains an amorphous collection of disparate case studies of unmade, unseen, and unreleased projects from across film and television history. There have been two dedicated edited collections on the subject—*Sights Unseen: Unfinished British Films* (2008) and *Shadow Cinema: The Historical and Production Contexts of Unmade Films* (2020)—with a further collection on the potential of unfinished women's films forthcoming (*Incomplete: The Feminist Possibilities of the Unfinished Film*). In addition, there have been several academic articles that have provided case studies of unmade or abandoned projects, most notably Peter Kunze's 'Herding *Cats*; or, the Possibilities of Unproduction Studies' (2020), in which the term unproduction studies was coined.

A variety of terms have been used to describe the field—lost, unproduced, unproduction, unmade, unseen, indirected, shadow cinema, phantom cinema, post-humous cinema, etc.—indicating the fledging nature of the discipline. Kunze's 'unproduction studies', a term devised in opposition to production studies, attempts to utilise the political economic framework of the latter in order to focus on below-the-line workers and to raise questions about 'hegemony, power, agency and resistance' within the film industries (Kunze 2020, 134). Production studies focuses on issues of labour, production, and authorial agency. Scholars like Miranda Banks et al. (2009) have focused their research on production cultures, hierarchies of labour, and the 'lived realities' of all those labourers involved in the production of film and television. It is an empirical field of enquiry, one based on observation, interviews, and archival sources and which focuses on constructing an understanding of the film and media industries from the bottom up, as opposed to industrially constructed accounts of corporations, companies, and institutions.

DOI: 10.4324/9781003206118-1

Kunze took the framework of production studies but questioned why it primarily focused on what was produced, asking, 'must media be produced to be studied?' (Kunze 2020, 131). He then applied the framework to a study of Steven Spielberg's unmade adaptation of the Broadway show *Cats* (1981). But Kunze's appropriation and inversion of production studies into unproduction studies did not necessarily define the object of study. Kunze relied on the idea of there being something available to produce and he initially relied on notions of success and failure: if something is not made, or produced, it is a failure, while something that is made or produced is a success. As he acknowledges in his case study of *Cats*, 'This area of inquiry not only should include projects that never made it to fruition, but unsuccessful attempts at successfully produced projects' (Kunze 2020, 129). I would agree. However, Kunze's use of the term 'successfully produced projects' can be misleading. After all, *Cats* was eventually produced as a feature film, not by Steven Spielberg but by Tom Hooper in 2019. Yet, to call the latter film a success given the barrage of negative critical attention it received and the fact it performed disastrously at the box office raises questions as to whether the film was more of a failure than a success. What I am suggesting is a need to be cautious in the use of the term failure in unproduction studies when discussing projects that are unmade. Just because a project was never produced does not automatically classify it as a failure. However, it can be an instructive object in uncovering the production cultures of creativity in film industries around the world as well as the ways in which film industries are typically built on an infrastructure of unmade projects: an entire system of writers, both professional and amateur, churning out ideas, scripts, and scenarios that are never, and will never, be made. Unproduction studies is not so much about failure as it is about creativity and the creative process and the archival methods that can be used to study it.

Maybe it is necessary to take a step back and consider the wider process of human creativity and how the majority of ideas do not even fail because they never even reach the point of being considered for publication or release, but rather...just come to nothing. Think of how many people, whether amateurs or not, have considered writing a novel or a script, set off on their ambition, only for it to fizzle into nothing: they grew bored, tired, found it impossible to complete, or realised writing a novel or script is actually quite hard. Or they might complete the novel or film script but have no intention of showing it to the world: they have written it for their own creative pleasure or for their friends.

Of course, there are 'amateurs' who write film scripts with the aim of breaking into the industry. Think of the number of scriptwriting manuals that exist, teaching budding screenwriters and directors the principles of how to write a script that will 'make it'. These manuals are nearly as old as the medium of film itself, with the earliest known manuals appearing in 1911 (Ralph Perkins Stoddard's *The Photo-Play: A Book of Valuable Information for Those Who Would Enter a Field of Unlimited Endeavour*) and 1913 (William Lewis Gordon's *How To Write Moving Pictures Plays*). These early manuals mitigated the expectations of the reader by making it clear that most screenplays would never be produced into a film. Take the opening statement to Gordon's revised edition of his manual: 'Neither do I wish to imply that by following these instructions ANYONE can become a successful photo playwright. This is not true. Everyone cannot succeed in any chosen profession' (Gordon 1914, 5). This is an early admission of the realities of the industrial system of creativity for budding film screenwriters. It is also a definition of success based on becoming a professional screenwriter able to make a sustained living. The realities of screenwriting have barely changed in the last one hundred years. Estimates suggests that each year anywhere between 25,000 and 50,000 unsolicited original 'spec scripts' flow through the main Hollywood companies (Myers 2012). Of them, an average of eighty-three a year are bought by a production company or agent, and of them only a fraction will ever be produced, with most entering protracted 'development hell' (Myers 2012). This suggests that upwards of 99 percent of all scripts remain unmade. These are only estimates and the figures are likely to fluctuate greatly in any given year. Most of the scripts will not only remain unmade, but also remain unread. And there are many more scripts and creative ideas that will not even enter this creative flow that sustains Hollywood. Perhaps even more sad is the fact that most of these scripts and creative ideas will never even be made available to an archive for later scholarly discovery. The scripts and ideas will simply disappear as if they never existed in the first place.

There needs to be a clear understanding that the boundaries and delineations between creative success and creative failure are not easy to mark. Certainly, any film that is produced and released is a success on one level: it made it through the system of development, production, distribution, and exhibition, despite whether it then goes on to fail commercially or critically. For the unproduction studies scholar, what is of interest is those films that are not made, produced, or realised and why that is the case. Why are so many projects left unmade?

The answer is not necessarily one of failure of individual projects and scripts. After all, given the abundance of scripts and creative ideas available versus the limited material resources available, it is inevitable that the majority of scripts and ideas will never be made. The large quantity of unmade projects is a reality of the film industries generally around the world rather than a reflection of 'failure'. As Kunze has subsequently argued, 'for this intriguing area of investigation to thrive, it must be liberal in its understanding of "failure" and sceptical of any perceived sharp distinction between unproduced and produced' (Kunze 2020, 130). Unproduction studies is a field that studies the process of creativity and development as much as it does the process of failure when writers, producers, directors, agents, or studio executives *do* attempt to produce a project. The projects Kunze outlines in his research certainly fall into the category of failure in one way or another: attempts were made by producers to realise a project, money was raised, but the projects collapsed.

However, the unproduction studies scholar will, on their travels through the archives of the world, come across many ideas and scripts that were left unmade simply because that is the nature of human creativity and the logic of the film industries. As a scholarly field, what we are investigating suggests a creative effort of some kind, but not necessarily that any traditional creative material exists, i.e. a screenplay. What the unproduction scholar will not easily discover are those script ideas that were discussed over a telephone, over a lunch, or between friends: many ideas are developed and shaped verbally, with no written record available. Unproduction studies also confronts the challenge posed by archival research in which there is often no linear and complete history of the unmade, merely creative debris and fragments. The object of study is unmade, skeletal, damaged, often non-existent. It is not in a form in which it can be easily moved from being unproduced to produced. It exists in a form utterly different to the object of study of classical film history. There is no complete film text and, quite often, no complete screenplay ready to enter production.

Unproduction studies is about exploring a shadowy archival world where little makes sense within the framework of existing canonical film history. Brian Norman, in his investigation of an unproduced James Baldwin script about the life of Malcolm X, captures the essence of the awkwardness of the unmade. He describes the object of study as a 'closet screenplay' and wonders how exactly it can be understood: 'The reading skills that literary studies offer this anomalous and necessarily politically charged bastard genre are limited given that there is no film, and therefore no film stills, to "read"' (Norman 2005, 103).

Simone Murray's investigations into the adaptation industry utilises the term 'phantom adaptations' to describe those films based on the literary property that were ultimately left unmade. Murray focuses on the unmade film adaptation of the novel *Eucalyptus* (1998) and how the screenplay that resulted offers the potential to problematise the entire field of adaptation studies, while the archival remains can provide 'fascinating insights into the functioning of the broader adaptation industry' (Murray 2008, 6).

Other academics have tentatively touched upon the unmade, usually only via career surveys of individual directors or screenwriters and often with an uncertainty of what was really being studied or what the unmade was actually about. But these outputs, and others like them, have indicated the potential of unproduction studies, including the theoretical dimensions of the field and the methods and approaches that can be utilised. So just what is unproduction studies? What does it involve? And why should it be taken seriously as a scholarly discipline? What follows is an attempt to answer these three questions in a bid to begin thinking through the potentialities of unproduction studies.

So what is unproduction studies?

As stated above, unproduction studies primarily involves archival research of unmade, unseen, or unreleased film and television projects that are typically (though, not exclusively) housed in archival institutions around the world. For the purposes of this study, I will be focusing on film. The predominant object of study are those projects that never even made it out of development, ranging from artistic documents (scripts, treatments, outlines, ideas scrawled on scraps of paper, photographs, location research, costume designs, artwork, even test footage), business documents, budgets, correspondence, readers' reports, studio ledgers, trade journal articles, and much more. An unmade project within the archive may not necessarily contain all of these items, as the case studies in this book make clear. Often an archive may make it apparent what unmade projects it contains via metadata in the archival catalogue. Other times, this is not the case, with material pertaining to the unmade distributed throughout other archival categories. So contingency is an inherent aspect in studying the unmade. One also needs to be mindful of the encounters with the unmade that resist archiving: the phone calls, the arguments, the discussions in corridors, and the thoughts in people's minds. All that remains of these encounters are archival fragments or people's (unreliable) memories, if that.

The unmade seems to be an integral part of how the media industries work. One reason for this is because of the nature of the creative process: ideas mutate and evolve, stories and scripts are developed and redeveloped, revised, and edited, to the point they become wholly new ideas and stories unrecognisable from the original idea. Draft one of a script will likely be very different to the final draft of the script. However, beyond this particular aspect of the creative process, there is clearly an expectation amongst producers and screenwriters that most projects will never be produced, particularly if they become stuck in 'development hell', a process in which a project (not necessarily even a screenplay, but maybe just a film title, a planned adaptation, or an elevator pitch) becomes trapped in a perpetual cycle of creation and revision for many years and usually leads to it eventually being abandoned, or even just left in a purgatory state.

In 2004, the then head of the UK Film Council's Development Fund, Jenny Borgars, described creative development as 'an agonisingly slow and frustrating process. "If you're developing a new project from scratch, you're fortunate if it takes two to three years, and it can take a lot longer"' (McNab 2004, 4). Seventy-three percent of the companies or producers that had received project development financing from the UK Film Council 'had failed to make a single film between them' (McNab 2004, 4). While this percentage relates to a specific funding scheme in the British film industry and therefore may reflect wider bureaucratic processes contributing to development hell, anecdotal evidence suggests that the unmade is a much bigger problem across film industries around the world. Filmmaker John Boorman reflected on the process of development hell as he had experienced it, stating that

> All film-makers spend time on aborted projects. [...] it is because the big studios play the destructive game of developing dozens of projects with the intention of making only one in ten or one in twenty. At any one time in Hollywood 90 per cent of the writers and directors are busy working on scripts that will not get made.
>
> (Boorman 1985, 21)

Peter Bart, reporting for *Variety*, noted how in a five-year period in the 2010s, only three projects out of fifty on one Hollywood studio's development slate had been produced (Bart 2013, 24).

The phrase development hell is not only common parlance within the film industry, but it has cut through to wider mainstream media, as reflected in David Hughes' bestselling *Tales from Development Hell*

(2003). Even a brief search of trade journal and newspaper databases reveals the preponderance of the term across the past forty years, as well as the longevity of some projects being trapped in development hell. Joy Horowitz, in 1987, published a story on the unmade *Forever*, a project that had been in perpetual development since the 1930s and was still being considered by producers in the late 1980s (Horowitz 1987). Development hell is not just an unfortunate circumstance to find oneself in, but a systemic industry problem, with production companies and even entire studios purposely enacting development hell strategies as a means of mitigating risk. There are even cycles of overdevelopment (putting into development more projects than can conceivably be produced) and underdevelopment (cutting back on the number of projects being put into development in order to reduce costs). Overdevelopment was a popular strategy among independent producers in the 1950s, who were dependent on studios for financing and therefore had to have a multiplicity of projects in development at any one time in readiness for a studio to give the greenlight on one of them (Fenwick 2020a, 22–23). In the early 1970s, due to an economic recession, many studios implemented brutal strategies of underdevelopment, cutting the funding to a range of projects that were already in the advanced stages of preproduction (Fenwick 2020b, 158–159).

The cyclical strategies of over- and underdevelopment continue in present-day Hollywood, with frequent stories in trade newspapers commenting on business trends at the major film production companies. In 2001, and then again in 2013, *Variety* reported on how development hell was 'freezing over' in Hollywood. What was meant by this was that major companies were initiating cost-cutting measures and therefore investing in fewer projects. In 2001, this was reported as meaning the following: 'Execs are avoiding taking chances. They prefer what they consider "slam-dunks," material that comes from established writers or with talent packages, and that is deemed ready to go out' (Lyons 2001, 1). In 2013, the freezing of development hell meant even stricter controls were put in place:

> 'Development slates have been compressed, meaning fewer projects, reduced writing fees and lower expectations from top management. [...] We are shortening the gap from the page to the stage,' reports another, meaning his studio has lost its enthusiasm for projects that drift through multiple drafts over several years in development hell. Studios increasingly are making one-draft deals with writers. The first try delivers or the project is cancelled.
>
> (Bart 2013, 4)

In 2000, *Variety* reported how Hollywood was heavily investing in the development of projects in anticipation of a writers' strike the following summer. The logic of this strategy was the fear of a lack of 'product flow' (Bart 2000, 4). So there appears to be an industrial logic (however perverse) behind the unmade, with cycles of overdevelopment and underdevelopment all predicated on the understanding of film production as being an inherently risky venture. This 'logic' was summed up by one anonymous production company executive in 2000:

> At the center of all this is the tacit admission that the studio development process is a total mess. The studios accept this and so do all those writers and filmmakers who wallow in development hell. It's absolutely amazing that the machinery of development, which is wasteful both of talent and money, has sustained itself this long. 'The whole process sucks,' the production chief of one studio told me last week. 'I hate it. Hate every aspect of it.' [...] In the end the wrong projects survive, representing perhaps less than 10% of those that were originally commissioned.
>
> (Bart 2000, 4)

Development hell, it would seem, is not a one-off process, but standard operating procedure for the film industry, with those projects that do get produced—and which constitute the canonical film history—being the privileged few. Most projects and ideas are simply left unmade. One cartoonist in *Variety* satirically depicted Satan sitting in his fiery office surrounded by a pile of scripts, while on his desk is a sign that reads 'development hell'. More specifically, a report by Paul Young in 1995 identified these gatekeepers as 'creative executives [...] they are a studio's first line of defense in the daily barrage of script submissions' (Young 1995, 1). The creative executive as a gatekeeper emerged in the mid-1980s in response to the rise of the so-called 'spec script': an unsolicited screenplay often submitted by, though not always, a first-time screenwriter, producer, or director looking to secure a development deal. Also employed by production companies and screen agencies are legions of script readers, often masters' degree graduates or aspiring screenwriters or producers. These script readers are asked to provide verdicts on the many hundreds of script submissions that companies and agencies receive by writing a brief synopsis and an analysis of plot, character, location, and market potential.

I too was once a script reader. I worked for several production companies and, for two years, with Northern Ireland Screen (NIS). The latter is the screen agency for Northern Ireland funded by the

Department for the Economy and the Department for Communities and oversees funds from the National Lottery. As part of my role at NIS, I was provided with extensive script training, including day-long courses on the three-act structure. Such training was led by people such as Ludo Smolski, an industry script 'doctor'—a noted screenwriter hired by producers and production companies to 'polish' an existing script—and facilitated by NIS development executives. The aim was to equip me and my fellow script readers with the skills to filter out scripts that were not deemed development-worthy because they infringed the accepted industry standards of screenwriting: whether formatting, poor characterisation, lack of theme, or underdeveloped plotting. I was being trained to gatekeep and uphold the standards of development.

Yet, not all projects that languish in development hell do so as a result of such gatekeeping, but rather because they are projects that are nothing more than a vague idea used to generate gossip and interest in a particular star, producer, or director. To be seen to be creative can be just as important as the actual process of creating, with an element of brand management being part of the process of floating potential film ideas in the trade press. Take the example of The Rolling Stones, a band that frequently flirted with potential film projects throughout the 1960s, most of which were not necessarily being given serious consideration. Maureen O'Grady, writing for *Rave* magazine, speculated as much in 1966 about The Rolling Stones' planned adaptation of the science fiction novel *Only Lovers Left Alive* (1964). She wondered if the project would 'ever be completed', and that 'it seems for as long as I can remember, the Stones have been making their film' (O'Grady 1966, 36). Though director Nicholas Ray was at one point rumoured to be involved in the project and writing a script, the project probably reflected more of a desire on behalf of the band's management to suggest a potential move into film production akin to The Beatles.

What is apparent is that the boundaries of unproduction studies are blurred and not necessarily easy to define. On the one extreme, there are projects that were produced in some form, but never achieved the full cycle necessary to become part of the official history of film and television. They remain absent in some way. On the other extreme, there are archival relics of paper and notes, unmade projects that challenge the very definition of what even constitutes a film project. Does a slim file with nothing but one piece of paper constitute an unmade film? Or does it require there to be a fully formed creative idea? And if so, what form must that creative idea take? Is it enough for a producer to consider an adaptation of a novel, for instance? Or does the producer need to have commissioned a writer to work up a treatment of the novel? In essence, these questions and extremes are fundamental to defining unproduction studies and the limitations of enquiry.

Questioning the boundaries of unproduction studies returns us to the issue of absence and nothingness that I briefly mentioned in the preface. Film and television studies are more secure in their status, with the object of study being clear: a produced film or television programme. Unproduction studies has the opposite problem: the absence of any clear object of study, both in history and in evidence, makes the field inherently insecure. At the same time, the intrinsic instability of unproduction studies is also its greatest potential as it offers the opportunity for scholars to reframe understanding of how film industries operate and the history of those films that do exist.

I am on the extreme end of unproduction studies as this book will make clear. I do not think that there has to be a firm script in existence for a project to be classed as unmade. I think it can be as simple as a project title, or even a title-less elevator pitch, or even just correspondence between creative labourers committing to collaborate on a project. The one prerequisite I do impose is that there has to be material evidence: so not quite nothing, but at least...something. It is a point previously made in the collection *Shadow Cinema* when setting out methods and approaches in the field: 'The paradigm for the study of shadow cinema and the unmade is that there must be a text of some kind, however simple and skeletal, that can form the basis of academic inquiry' (Fenwick et al. 2020, 6).

The reason I impose this requirement for archival evidence is because unproduction studies is a field primarily concerned with the material, social, and cultural conditions of production. While the study of the unmade does pose philosophical questions about the nature of film texts, it is not itself a philosophical discipline. It is concerned with how film industries operate, the way projects are developed and produced, and why it is that creative projects are more likely *not* to be produced. The discipline is working towards a wider research goal: to uncover the extent of the unmade across film history and the scale to which it underpins film industries, evidence of which can be found in archives. But archives never provide linear, ready-to-write histories. They are inconsistent, contested, and filled with gaps and absences. Archives usually will only contain one perspective and the unproduction studies scholar will at some point be required to undertake detective work in order to trace the archive trail left behind by the unmade. This is exactly why I believe it is necessary to have extreme boundaries when it comes to defining unproduction studies. For while it may well be that one archive contains a single piece of paper with nothing more than a film title (if that), sustained research may eventually lead to the discovery of material evidence across a range of archival repositories in what amounts to substantial creative material.

What does unproduction studies involve?

Unproduction studies involves efforts to map and understand this history of the unmade within the archive, as well as work towards reimagining the unmade through innovative means of creative practice. These efforts ensure that unproduction studies is naturally multidisciplinary. The core of the work involves archival research, but the field is rather divergent on methods and approaches at present given that it is still finding its way. Some film and media historians have utilised unmade projects to study the careers of individual filmmakers. This includes work on the unmade films of Stanley Kubrick, with scholars such as Peter Krämer and Filippo Ulivieri (2021) surveying those projects never made to understand their relationship with the films Kubrick did produce. This approach aims to complicate the existing histories of such filmmakers and to scrutinise the material conditions of production. Others have taken this approach, but with a more emphatic use of the unmade to make wider points about political contexts, such as Larry Ceplair's (2019) career survey of screenwriter Ring Lardner, Jr. Throughout his study, Ceplair forcefully uses the phrase 'it was not made' time and again in a bid to demonstrate the struggles Lardner endured and the career low points he suffered as a result of the blacklist in the USA in the 1950s. The use of unmade projects to study such political barriers to success is further highlighted in Whitney Strub's survey of playwright, poet, and activist Amiri Baraka. Strub argues that the study of the unmade (and also the unseen)

> enriches the Baraka narrative in a number of ways, from grounding his vision of cultural politics in the very concrete setting of late-sixties Newark and San Francisco, to contextualizing the heavily cinematic aesthetics of some of his Marxist plays.
>
> (Strub 2015, 273)

It's a sentiment echoed by Lars Lierow in his case study of the unfinished documentary *Revolution in Black America* by the Black Arts Movement. Just as Ceplair and Strub aim to uncover structural forces that have marginalised filmmaking voices, Lierow equally aims to restore a hidden history, seeing the potential for the unmade, 'to write the Black Arts Movement into the history of black cinema and reopen the question of a black cinematic aesthetic' (2013, 3).

Building on the career assessment approach is Christopher Sieving (2011) who surveys an entire genre—blaxploitation—rather than just an individual filmmaker. Sieving presents a case study of the unproduced *The Confessions of Nat Turner* alongside produced films to understand the evolution of blaxploitation in the 1960s and 1970s. Kieran Foster (2019) takes Sieving's approach one step further, focusing on not only a genre, but the output of an entire production company, in his study of horror and Hammer Productions. Some have utilised case studies of the unmade in an attempt towards revisionist histories of entire national film industries, such as David Welky's (2006) exploration of MGM's unmade *The Forty Days of Musa Dagh*, which he relates to wider forces of an internationalised post-World War Two Hollywood. Welky's case study is grounded in a historical analysis not only of the conditions of production, but also of the historical events being portrayed. Such an approach has been adopted by others, such as Geoffrey Ellis (2009) in his study of Stanley Kubrick's unmade script *Napoleon*.

Other scholars have used the unmade in order to theorise the concept of failure in the cultural industries. It's an approach taken, as discussed above, by Kunze (2018) in his study of the failed attempt to adapt *Gone with the Wind* as a Broadway musical. Kunze argues that the study of failed adaptations and the unmade indicates the wider 'generative possibilities' of unproduction studies to understand how the film industry operates (2018, 802). Equally, I. Q. Hunter has emphasised these generative possibilities, arguing that

> a more expansive understanding of unmade films, taking it into post-structuralist territory, would emphasise that all films were at some point unmade and that tracing their production uncovers possible alternative versions later discarded, compromised, or unrealised; it would show how films are haunted by the ghosts of their own production history and that released films are palimpsests of their unrealised versions.
>
> (2018)

The unmade, in other words, offers a wide-ranging scope to understand textual, structural, and industrial dimensions of films and the film industry as of yet untouched (at least, not in any substantive way) by film and media studies.

But unproduction studies does not just involve theoretical or historical research, but it also involves creative practitioners that use the debris of the unmade to construct new works of art or to think through imagined possibilities of what might have been. Artists Jane and Louise Wilson conducted archival research of Stanley Kubrick's unmade *Aryan Papers*, which served as the inspiration to their video installation, *Unfolding the Aryan Papers* (2009). The artists outlined their motivations as follows:

> Fascinated by this project that never came to be, they combed through Kubrick's research and sought out the actress he had cast for the lead role, Johanna ter Steege. *Unfolding the Aryan Papers* combines Kubrick's research images and original wardrobe stills with footage of ter Steege shot by the artists. It is at once a documentary resurrection of the abandoned film, a portrait of the actress, a response to Kubrick's working method, and an exploration of the unrepresentable nature of the Holocaust.
>
> (Courtauld n.d.)

Other creative practitioners have investigated ways of building empathetic bridges between the archival remains of the unmade and film audiences. A colleague at Sheffield Hallam University, filmmaker Chris Cooke, took this approach when staging live script readings of unmade Hammer films at the Mayhem Film Festival in Nottingham. Wanting to rely on the audiences' imagination, Cooke, in collaboration with fellow filmmaker Steven Sheil, decided to stage the readings in the cinema auditorium. Throughout the reading, the cinema screen largely remained blank, apart from the occasional still image to serve as a transitional cue. The aim was for the audience to project their own desired image of the unmade film onto the cinema screen, while the actors remained to the side of the auditorium. Cooke had to write a screenplay given that only film treatments existed. Cooke's approach is echoed in a series of radio stage plays for BBC Radio 4 entitled *Unmade Movies* (2018), which brought to life unmade films such as Alfred Hitchcock's *The Blind Man*.

The scale of the challenge facing unproduction studies scholars is profound, with an institution like the Margaret Herrick Library alone containing over 17,000 records clearly identified as unproduced films. And that is just *one* archival repository. There is an untapped global research resource that can uncover hidden histories of the film industries of all nations.

Why should unproduction studies be taken so seriously?

I would suggest that there are two distinct issues at stake in unproduction studies: the structural and the textual. The former considers the questions of barriers to production and of who or what the gatekeepers are within the film industries. The latter raises questions as to how the unmade can be defined and what even constitutes the unmade. Together, the structural and the textual challenge the very foundations of existing film and television history.

The textual concerns the unfinished state of the unmade and raises questions as to how to make sense of this material and reconstruct it. These textual questions arise out of the study of the unfinished within literary studies (Allen 2015; Beeston 2018). Beyond the humanities, the body of work on the unfinished, unmade, unrealised, including in engineering, architecture, geography, etc., is expansive (Carse and Kneas 2019; Harle 2018). Matilda Bathurst raises the intriguing point that 'the growing trend for celebrating the "unmade" raises interesting philosophical questions about current attitudes to material culture' (2012, 54). Certainly, these are fundamental questions as to what is being studied within unproduction studies. What are the objects of enquiry and what are we trying to find out? Andrew Spicer argues that in studying unmade films, scholars are 'deliberately problematising the object of study, what we might mean by a "film text"' (Spicer 2010, 299). Unmade films are usually material artefacts predominantly confined to the archive. Even when attempting to recreate an unmade film, it is through the refashioning of those material remnants into a new creative object (whether an academic article or an art installation).

The challenge for unproduction studies is about how to relate the textual dimensions of the unmade to wider structural forces: the gatekeepers and barriers within the industry that decide what gets produced and what is left unmade. The fact that, for example, Stanley Kubrick's archive is filled with scraps of ideas is no surprise and really does not tell us much at all. My own hard drive and notepad is filled with ideas and tasks that will always remain unfinished. The same will apply to you. The interesting question, however, is the sheer number of creative ideas that exist in the Kubrick archive in a much more fully realised form. When one considers the materiality of the unmade and the empirical evidence available, it is possible to begin investigating how the textual and the structural are absolutely linked. After all, *why* did a producer that ultimately became as successful as Kubrick have so many projects that remained unmade? Was he unique in this regard or does it suggest a wider systematic pattern of creative behaviour across the industry?

Embedded within the film industry are inherent inequalities and barriers that have ensured that women, more often than men, struggle to successfully produce films. As Shelley Cobb has argued, 'just writing about the films women filmmakers do make leaves out whole portions of women's film history [...] there are women's films throughout film history that have never been made. And these unmade films also have a history' (Cobb 2014). Similarly, there is a history of unmade films by LGBTQ+ and persons of colour, films that remained unmade because of the structural inequalities and industrial gatekeepers. The recent wave of demonstrations against the Academy Awards for a lack of diverse representation—culminating with #OscarsSoWhite trending on Twitter—can be more fully understood through the prism of the unmade and structural barriers. In a discussion of the emergence of a wave of Black American filmmakers in Hollywood in the early 1990s (Spike Lee, Hudlin Brothers, John Singleton, Mario Van Peebles, Charles Lane, Matty Rich), Reggie Ugwu outlines how many of the directors, after an initial successfully produced film each, were subsequently marginalised and found it difficult to move a project out of development and into production. Through a series of interviews, Ugwu reveals the struggles and barriers faced by many Black American filmmakers (though, of course, not all) by the end of the 1990s:

> As the decade wore on, a wall was re-erected, black filmmakers now say, and many of the same people who had been held up as the faces of a changing industry watched as their careers ground slowly to a halt. 'I was told that I was in director's jail,' said Matty Rich.
>
> (director of *Straight Outta Brooklyn*, 1991) (Ugwu 2019)

Filmmaker Darnell Martin has argued that Black American filmmakers in the 1990s had been set up to fail; that their later unmade projects were a result of inherent structural racism; and that the brief window of opportunity was merely an opportunity for studio executives 'to pat themselves on the back like they did something' (Ugwu 2019). The endemic nature of these structural inequalities was recently highlighted in research by Stacy Smith, who investigated representation and inclusivity both on and off screen in Hollywood. The findings revealed that 'across 1,223 directors over 11 years, 4.3 percent were female, 5.2 percent were Black or African-American and 3.1 percent were Asian or Asian-American' (USC Annenberg Staff 2018). Whitney Strub has argued that the key issue in studying the unmade is to uncover and bring attention to these structural barriers, stating, 'these unrealized films do much to enrich our understanding of the conditions of possibility for Black cinema' (Strub 2015, 274). More importantly, the study of the unmade films of Black American filmmakers 'recovers another lost piece of black film history' (Strub 2015, 284). There is, however, much more work to be done in this regard.

Unproduction studies has many vital goals, then, including to uncover the history of unmade films from across marginalised and underrepresented communities. As Cobb has stressed, the danger of not studying the unmade is the potential erasure of large portions of film history, particularly those histories of overlooked individuals and communities (Cobb 2014). Unproduction studies is a field that has the potential to highlight the patterns of structural barriers across history. All of these issues (which also include censorship, political sensitivities, cultural conditions, production financing, etc.) lead to the discussion of marginalisation and absences, for current film history and archive methods privilege produced films, with an oversight of the unmade.

Archives and archival methods

There are gaps and absences in archives of the unmade, and ultimately in the history of the unmade that unproduction studies is trying to construct. Therefore, questions about how unproduction studies can approach the archive from new perspectives, rather than relying on approaches that privilege the produced, are vital. Unproduction studies has the radical potential to challenge canonical history by foregrounding the marginalised and the forgotten in the archive. But to do so, I would suggest that the unmade scholar has to take on the role of what Lynée Lewis Gaillet calls the 'stance of archivist-researcher' (2012, 35). Gaillet makes it clear that the use of archives requires a constant process of reflection and critique on archival methods. There has been a recent upsurge in calls for scholars to collaborate closely with archivists, rather than work *against* archivists, i.e. assuming that the archivist and the archive is at the service of the academic. Oliver Hanley and Adelheid Heftberger talk of the potential, 'synergy, collaboration, interdisciplinary research, and mutual benefit' in the archivist/scholar relationship (2012, 65), while Ralph Kingston urges scholars to focus more on the materiality of the archive in terms of how it came to be: its material history or the 'specifics of its material or institutional embodiment' (2011, 1). The common theme across this output of reflection on archival methods is materiality and the process of using the archive, or the 'doing of history'. Barbara L'Eplattenier makes the point that archival methods are rarely discussed, but instead disguised and hidden from the process of researching and writing history:

> Why do we not have articles about finding aids? About searching databases? About organizing and using sources? About verifying information? Why do we as a discipline rarely talk about the methods we use to access our information? How might we incorporate such information into our research?
>
> (L'Eplattenier 2009, 67–68)

I am not suggesting that these arguments are new. As L'Eplattenier highlights, there are periodic cycles of scholarly despair at archival methods and a basic lack of archival training on doctoral programmes (2009, 68). Rather, the point is to stress the process of self-reflexivity and methodological transparency as the field of unproduction studies progresses. In order to study and understand the unmade, it is necessary to use archives. Indeed, the study of the unmade is *about* archives and the material they contain and as such one cannot separate the materiality of the unmade from the archive. The process of archival investigation should therefore be at the front and centre of unproduction studies research, making it clear what archives are being consulted, how they came into existence, and the material conditions of the archival data set (size, condition, subsequent additions to the collection, etc.). If unproduction studies is about utilising overlooked archival material—the forgotten and the marginalised—then it is necessary to underline why it was forgotten and what the material can and can't reveal. In short, unproduction studies research needs to talk about the archive. Such explicit reflexivity, both in process and in output, is exactly the performative stance Gaillet urges academics to adopt (2012, 54). Both archivists and academics perform a dual role in the archive as archivist-researchers, involved in a constant process of contextualisation and re-contextualisation, but the process requires transparency, with the researcher outlining exactly what is being counted as evidence. This is hugely important in unproduction studies. The study of the unmade requires us to ask what is being used to reconstruct the history of the unmade. What material is being used towards highlighting absences and gaps? And what material is also being ignored or overlooked?

As I mentioned in the preface, I came to unproduction studies out of a distraction for material that defied standard cataloguing procedures: creative debris, the failed notes, scribbles, half-finished scripts, and so on. But much of this material was 'off' catalogue (with catalogues typically constructed to favour the produced) and so required me to develop a collaborative relationship with the archivists at the archival institution in order to ascertain what was *not* on the public-facing catalogue. Alexis Ramsey makes the point that there are often 'hidden' archives that an archivist-researcher must come to terms with, and that 'most archives have more unprocessed or partially processed collections than they do fully processed collections, creating, in effect, three distinct archives—the hidden, the partially hidden or partially processed, and the visible archive' (Ramsey 2010, 79).

Archives are in a constant process of evolution, whether it is because they are still being catalogued or receiving new material. Indeed, some scholars will actively catalogue a collection on behalf of an institution. But in utilising uncatalogued archives, scholars should once again be transparent about the process, foregrounding how it transforms historical knowledge and the material dimensions of why such knowledge has been overlooked or forgotten. Matthew Harle discusses how the marginalisation of the unmade is often a result of cataloguing procedures:

> Archives are spaces where abandoned texts go un-described or are compiled alongside a completed project. [...] it is likely that if an abandoned or unfinished project is foregrounded in archival description, it is most probably because of the significance of its creator, or its relation to a publicly known text. This means that principally, the abandoned work suffers from a crude selectivity of the canonicity of the creator.
>
> (Harle 2018, 29)

A reflection on catalogues and cataloguing can reveal much about the shape and materiality of an archive, as well as processes of gatekeeping and hidden histories. As Gaillet has argued, the inherent chaos of many archives can prohibit discovery and access, leading to institutionalised marginalisation (2012, 53). If research demand is for typically canonical directors or films, limited funding and appropriately trained staff may necessitate the prioritisation of those collections being effectively catalogued, with other collections being marginalised.

Archivists and researchers are the principal gatekeepers of archives, being the predominant users of them. But at the same time, 'traditional notions of gatekeeping' can be abandoned by a focus on materiality, method, and process (Gaillet 2012, 54). It is the fundamental point of using and revisiting archives, to ensure that, as Glenn and Enoch argue, 'histories do change—in response to the dominant values of institutions, cultures, and historiographers (history writers) themselves' (Glenn and Enoch 2009, 321). The archive and archival research should not be static, but be constantly evolving, with identities and knowledge being reshaped through the role of the archivist-researcher. In unproduction studies, it is also a process of not only revisiting canonical or dominant archival sites, but also locating new sites or archives outside of the mainstream.

The point I am trying to make here is how the study of unmade film and television cannot and should not be told without explicit reference to the material existence of the object of study or of the archival institutions in which it is held. Method and approach, I would suggest, have to be not only at the forefront of unproduction studies research, but an absolute vital component, without which it undermines the objectives of recovering the marginalised and forgotten. For L'Eplattenier, archival methods and approaches should be embedded into our research from the development phase as they are 'the means by which we conduct our research, how we locate and use primary materials, and for historians, how we recover materials for our histories' (2009, 69). This is not to lament current unproduction studies research or to suggest unproduction studies scholars do not consider archive methods and materiality. But an open discussion about how unproduction studies scholars use archives, the lived experience of archivist-researchers, and how to locate the unmade when it is so often hidden is surely a key process in the study of unmade film and television. Unproduction studies scholars should not be afraid as historians to document the process of doing history, but rather celebrate the transparency and openness of the research methods used and sources consulted (or ignored). In their discussion of the construction of history, specifically film history, Monica Dall'asta and Jane Gaines contest the very notion of the term history, asking whether it is 'a production ambiguity (the history of the history) or a highly ideological conflation, an operation that conceals the fact of the construction of an interpretative narrative' (2015, 14). And this is a key point: in recovering the histories of the unmade, I would argue it is first necessary to understand that history *within* the archive, not subsuming it and the sources into existing canonical history and methodological approaches.

Unproduction studies is closely aligned with the methods and approaches of the new film history. New film history emphasises the role of the archive and primary sources in understanding the institutional practices of the film industry (Chapman et al. 2009). The aim is to situate existing knowledge of film history within wider social, political, and industrial contexts, while both production and reception of films are emphasised. But what has been overlooked by the new film history are unmade film and television projects. Instead, it has to date privileged the produced over the unproduced, with the new film history using the archive to study that which exists. New film history research that does engage with the unmade typically aligns it with existing, known histories, film texts, or canonical figures, thereby further privileging the produced. Unproduction studies should engage with the material existence of archival evidence of the unmade first in order to reframe the study of film and media industries away from traditional notions of success and failure and to foreground the creative process.

The history of the unmade should be a counter history to challenge existing film history, with the gaps and absences not being resolved. I believe that unproduction studies scholars need to coordinate efforts towards relating empirical microhistory case studies of the unmade (whether of canonical directors or of the marginalised voices of women, Black, Asian, and Minority Ethnic, LGBTQ+ filmmakers) to a macrohistory of Hollywood and other film industries that consider the structural forces at work and the cultural and industrial logic behind the unmade. Therefore, unproduction studies can work towards a counter history that challenges existing assumptions about how film and media industries work, how producers and production companies operate, and why film and media history has privileged some over others. As argued in *Shadow Cinema*,

> Perhaps we've been asking ourselves the wrong questions for far too long. Instead of thinking about why a film was made, we should be asking why so many films were never made and think about the implications of the Hollywood that might have been.
> (Fenwick et al. 2020, 7)

The potential of unproduction studies is in its fundamental concern with structural forces. This is not to dismiss the new film history and its achievements, but to suggest unproduction studies can complement existing research, while working towards a revisionist, counter history. Counter in the sense that the prevailing discourse within film and media history remains on how Hollywood *does* work, with a focus on the produced. Unproduction studies reframes this discourse, still considering how Hollywood *does* work, but with a focus on the unproduced.

The plan of action for unproduction studies going forward involves the need for a deeper reflection on archival methods. Gaillet, in the discussion of the performativity of the archivist-researcher, proposes the following challenges:

> (1) revisiting primary and canonical materials with a new set of research questions in mind, (2) mining a broader range of archives than heretofore considered, (3) viewing (and adding to existing) archives in ways that make knowledge rather than simply finding what's already known, and (4) taking advantage of new technologies to expand the scope and possibilities inherent in archival investigation.

These challenges seem wholly appropriate to unproduction studies, particularly in order to consider questions of absences, materiality, and marginalisation. But the challenges also link back to the need for greater self-reflexivity, particularly in the consideration of a 'broader range of archives'; the unproduction studies scholar and community arguably needs to work towards a mapping exercise of archives and primary sources in order to understand both the scale and the location of the unmade in archives around the world. But perhaps it is also necessary to call into question the reliance on institutional archives and to consider how the unmade is often hidden. What of, for example, contemporary examples of the unmade, which will largely be generated digitally? How is this being archived and what are the implications for future research? Does the unproduction studies scholar need to go beyond archival institutions and commence ethnographic studies, observing screenwriters or script readers at film agencies? Is there a need to forge relationships with production companies in order to access private archives? Indeed, there are arguably existing online archives of the unmade at websites such as The Black List (https://blcklst.com/) and The Brit List (https://brit-list.co.uk/), each of which provides annual lists of the best unproduced screenplays. There are anonymous individuals that have decided to 'leak' the unproduced files of studios. This is the case with the Twitter account 'Paramount Unproduced Properties 1983–1997', created in May 2020. The anonymous account holder acquired access to the unproduced files of Paramount Pictures and releases them daily. How is one able to make sense of this material, both practically (the scale) and also ethically? In contrast, there are industry figures that openly and legally release their unproduced work online, such as director and screenwriter David Koepp. His website contains PDFs of scripts that were not produced (David Koepp n.d.).

New technologies are also presenting new opportunities for research. Many archival institutions have begun a process of digitisation, making elements of collections available digitally and online. The digital archive has been of vital importance to the case studies in this book, making archival research feasible during the coronavirus pandemic of 2020–2021. However, the process of digitising archives can be highly selective. Those documents that are frequently handled or fragile benefit first from new digital scanning technologies, but this may in itself reinforce canonical materials that are the most requested by researchers, further marginalising the unmade. It becomes yet another process of gatekeeping, one in which archivists and institutions ascribe greater value to particular documents and collections, with the archive becoming the 'institutionalized arbiter of value' (Ramsey 2010, 84). The dangers of digitisation (along with the potentialities) is once more indicative of the need for greater collaboration between academics and archivists, and a much wider discussion is needed across universities and archival institutions about the gatekeeping and structural reinforcement of privileged histories.

Conclusion

This chapter has provided an extended consideration of unproduction studies and its recent developments, as well as a survey of some of the most pertinent debates that are taking place. Given that it is still such a fledgling field of enquiry within film and media studies means there is still much that is unknown and many questions to be explored in terms of methods and approaches. The chapter's focus on foregrounding archival methods is crucial for the evolution of the field and, as such, archival methods are at the heart of the remainder of this book.

What follows is a case study of one particular archival collection, the Production Code Administration (PCA) records, and a study of the unmade films within it. The case study details the methods for analysing the PCA records, understanding them first and foremost as archival objects that exist within an institution, the Margaret Herrick Library. As previously stated, rather than the case study being a history of the PCA, it is about contributing to the broader goal of understanding and locating the unmade within archives as well as looking to ascertain the structural forces that lead to projects remaining unmade. Surprisingly, what is revealed is that the PCA was quite often *not* the structural barrier to production, but rather a wider array of contexts, factors, organisations, and individuals. The archival collection consists of production files submitted to the PCA, which the PCA filed away, but each of the projects has a unique history and story to tell, quite often one distinct from anything to do with the PCA. The production files typically consist of documents and correspondence that have nothing to do with the PCA, but which have simply come to be archived within the PCA records. However, before I discuss the archival collection itself, the next chapter will provide a brief contextual history of the PCA to understand why these documents came to exist within its archive.

Works cited

Allen, James R. 2015. 'What Is an Unfinished Work?' *New Literary History* 46, no. 1: 125–142.

Banks, Mirana, Mayer, Vicki, and Caldwell, John, eds. 2009. *Production Studies: Cultural Studies of Media Industries*. New York: Routledge.

Bart, Peter. 2000. 'Dog Days in Development Hell'. *Variety* 380, no. 2: 4, 128.

———. 2013. 'Development Hell Freezes Over'. *Variety* 320, no. 13: 24.

Bathurst, Matilda. 2012. 'What Remains?: Paper Architecture and the World of the Unmade'. *The World of Antiques & Art* no. 82: 54–57.

Beeston, Alix. 2018. *In and Out of Sight: Modernist Writing and the Photographic Unseen*. New York: Oxford University Press.

Boorman, John. 1985. *Money into Light: The Emerald Forest: A Diary*. London: Faber and Faber.

Carse, Ashley and Kneas, David. 2019. 'Unbuilt and Unfinished: The Temporalities of Infrastructure'. *Environment and Society: Advances in Research* 10, no. 1: 9–28.

Ceplair, Larry. 2019. 'Ring Lardner, Jr. and the Hollywood Blacklist: A New Perspective on the Perennial Struggle against Thought Control in the United States'. *Historical Journal of Film, Radio and Television* 39, no. 1: 75–95.

Chapman, James, Glancy, Mark, and Harper, Sue, eds. 2009. *New Film History: Sources, Methods, Approaches*. Basingstoke: Palgrave Macmillan.

Cobb, Shelley. 2014. 'Women Directors and Lost Projects'. https://womensfilmandtelevisionhistory.wordpress.com/2014/03/21/women-directors-and-lost-projects/.

Courtauld. N.d. 'Jane and Louise Wilson: Unfolding the Aryan Papers'. https://courtauld.ac.uk/gallery/what-on/exhibitions-displays/ma-curating-archive/the-second-hand-reworked-art-over-time/jane-and-louise-wilson-unfolding-the-aryan-papers.

Dall'asta, Monica and Gaines, Jane. 2015. 'Prologue. Constellations: Past Meets Present in Feminist Film History'. In *Doing Women's Film History: Reframing Cinemas, Past and Future*, edited by Christine Gledhill and Julia Knight, 13–25. Chicago: University of Illinois Press.

David Koepp. n.d. https://davidkoepp.com/script-archive/.

Ellis, Geoffrey. 2009. 'Stanley Kubrick's "Napoleon": A Historian's Critique of the Screenplay'. In *Stanley Kubrick's Napoleon*, edited by Alison Castle, 237–249. Cologne: Taschen.

Fenwick, James. 2020a. 'A Production Strategy of Overdevelopment: Kirk Douglas's Bryna Productions and the Unproduced *Viva Gringo!*' In *Shadow Cinema: The Historical and Production Contexts of Unmade Films*, edited by James Fenwick, Kieran Foster, and David Eldridge, 17–37. New York: Bloomsbury.

Fenwick, James. 2020b. *Stanley Kubrick Produces*. New Brunswick, NJ: Rutgers University Press.

Fenwick, James, Foster, Kieran, and Eldridge, David. 2020. 'Introduction'. In *Shadow Cinema: The Historical and Production Contexts of Unmade Films*, edited by James Fenwick, Kieran Foster, and David Eldridge, 1–14. New York: Bloomsbury.

Foster, Kieran. 2019. *Unseen Horrors: The Unmade Films of Hammer*. PhD thesis, De Montfort University.

Gaillet, Lynée L. 2012. '(Per)Forming Archival Research Methodologies'. *College Composition and Communication* 64, no. 1: 35–58.

Glenn, Cheryl and Enoch, Jessica. 2009. 'Drama in the Archives: Rereading Methods, Rewriting History'. *College Composition and Communication* 61, no. 2: 321–342.

Gordon, William L. 1914. *How to Write Moving Picture Plays*. Cincinnati, OH: Atlas Publishing Company.

Hanley, Oliver and Heftberger, Adelheid. 2012. 'Scholarly Archivists/Archival Scholars: Rethinking the Traditional Models'. *The Velvet Light Trap* no. 70: 64–65.

Harle, Matthew. 2018. *Afterlives of Abandoned Work: Creative Debris in the Archive*. London: Bloomsbury.

Horowitz, Joy. 1987. 'Development Hell'. *American Film* 13, no. 2: 53–55.

Hunter, I.Q. 2018. 'Researching Unmade Films: Who Cares and Why Bother?' Conference paper presented at CATHI Conference, October 31.

Kingston, Ralph. 2011. 'The French Revolution and the Materiality of the Modern Archive'. *Libraries & the Cultural Record* 46, no. 1: 1–25.

Krämer, Peter and Ulivieri, Filippo. 2021. 'Kubrick's Unrealized Projects'. In *The Bloomsbury Companion to Stanley Kubrick*, edited by Nathan Abrams and I.Q. Hunter, 327–335. New York: Bloomsbury.

Kunze, Peter. 2018. 'Belles are Singing: Broadway, Hollywood, and the Failed *Gone with the Wind* Musical'. *Historical Journal of Film, Radio and Television* 38, no. 4: 787–807.

———. 2020. 'Herding *Cats*; or the Possibilities of Unproduction Studies'. In *Shadow Cinema: The Historical and Production Contexts of Unmade Films*, edited by James Fenwick, Kieran Foster, and David Eldridge, 129–151. New York: Bloomsbury.

L'Eplattenier, Barbara, E. 2009. 'Opinion: An Argument for Archival Research Methods: Thinking Beyond Methodology'. *College English* 72, no. 1: 67–69.

Lierow, Lars. 2013. '"The Black Man's Vision of the World": Rediscovering Black Arts Filmmaking and the Struggle for a Black Cinematic Aesthetic'. *Black Camera* 4, no. 2: 3–21.

Lyons, Charles. 2001. 'Development Hell Freezing over?' *Variety* 382, no. 1: 1, 71.

McNab, Geoffrey. 2004. 'Development Hell'. *Sight & Sound* 14, no. 9: 4–5.

Murray, Simone. 2008. 'Phantom Adaptations: *Eucalyptus*, the Adaptation Industry and the Film That Never Was'. *Adaptation* 1, no. 1: 5–23.

Myers, Scott. 2012. 'The Definitive Spec Script Deals List: 1998'. June 14. https://gointothestory.blcklst.com/the-definitive-spec-script-sales-list-1991-2012-1998-918113f4199a.

Norman, Brian. 2005. 'Reading a "Closet Screenplay": Hollywood, James Baldwin's Malcolms and the Threat of Historical Irrelevance'. *African American Review* 39, no. 1–2: 103–118.

O'Grady, Maureen. 1966. 'The Most Expensive Film Never Made?' *Rave* no. 33: 36.

Ramsey, Alexis E. 2010. 'Viewing the Archives: The Hidden and the Digital'. In *Working in the Archives: Practical Research Methods for Rhetoric and Composition*, edited by Alexis E. Ramsey, Wendy B. Sharer, Barbara L'Eplattenier, and Lisa S. Mastrangelo, 79–90. Carbondale: Southern Illinois University Press.

Sieving, Christopher. 2011. *Soul Searching: Black-Themed Cinema from the March on Washington to the Rise of Blaxploitation*. Middletown, CT: Wesleyan University Press.

Spicer, Andrew. 2010. 'Creativity and Commerce: Michael Klinger and New Film History'. *New Review of Film and Television Studies* 8, no. 3: 297–314.

Strub, Whitney. 2015. 'The Baraka Film Archive: The Lost, Unmade, and Unseen Film Work of LeRoi Jones/Amiri Baraka'. *Black Camera* 7, no. 1: 273–287.

Ugwu, Reggie. 2019. '"They Set Us Up to Fail": Black Directors of the '90s Speak Out'. *New York Times*, July 3. https://www.nytimes.com/2019/07/03/movies/black-directors-1990s.html.

USC Annenberg Staff. 2018. https://news.usc.edu/147111/diversity-in-hollywood-remains-unchanged-stacy-smith/.

Welky, David. 2006. 'Global Hollywood versus National Pride: The Battle to Film *The Forty Days of Musa Dagh*'. *Film Quarterly* 59, no. 3: 35–43.

Young, Paul. 1995. 'Development Hell Now Looks Like Kids' Stuff'. *Variety* 359, no. 8: 1.

2 Hollywood and the Production Code Administration

The Production Code Administration (PCA) records are housed at the Margaret Herrick Library in Los Angeles. As stated, the aim is to use the collection to survey a sample of unmade projects contained in the Margaret Herrick Library Digital Collections to understand why they were not made. As will become clear in later chapters, what the survey finds is that a number of the projects that have been designated as 'unproduced' in the PCA records were themselves deemed acceptable for production by the PCA, therefore indicating other reasons for the projects never being realised. That said, with this chapter I want to provide a brief contextual overview of the PCA, of its relationship with the Hollywood studios, and of scholarly research into the organisation in order to understand why it is that the PCA records contain extensive archival documentation of unmade films. The chapter also provides a general overview of how Hollywood and the mainstream American film industry found and developed stories during the period in which the PCA was in existence, between the 1930s and early 1960s.

Hollywood and production

The studio system, the era from approximately the 1920s through to the 1950s, was a time in which Hollywood was dominated by the 'major' studios: MGM, Warner Bros., RKO, Fox Film Corporation (renamed Twentieth Century-Fox in 1935), Paramount, Universal, Columbia, and United Artists. Most of the majors exclusively contracted creative labourers—directors, producers, screenwriters, cinematographers, actors, etc.—and formalised the process of creativity into a hierarchy of production. Termed the producer unit system, management was centralised within the role of the producer 'in which a group of men [producers] supervised six to eight films per year, usually each producer concentrating on a particular type of film' (Bordwell

DOI: 10.4324/9781003206118-2

et al. 1985, 559). This hierarchy of creative power and organisation led to what Thomas Schatz called a 'consistent system of production', what amounted to a conveyor belt of film development, production, distribution, and exhibition (Schatz 2010, 6). Existing histories of the production processes of the Hollywood studio system, such as those by Bordwell, Staiger, and Thompson and Schatz emphasise the specialisation of creative labour, the standardisation of production, and of what Ronny Regev calls the 'streamlining of creative production' (2016, 593). Creativity was a highly controlled internal process at the studios, with ideas and scripts being developed by multiple individuals and with input from a range of writers, the director, and of course the producer, with the latter sanctioning ideas.

Claus Tieber's (2014) research on the working life of industry professional screenwriters (those that were contracted to a particular studio or production company and were members of the Writers Guild of America) during the studio system era brings to light the realities of creative development. Stories and scripts would be developed via a conferencing system, in which all the key players in a particular producer unit would come together and discuss the latest iteration of a script. Tieber's research aligns with the work of Schatz in stressing that creativity was not the result of one individual, but of the system itself. As Tieber's research makes clear, all ideas and scripts had to pass through this conferencing system within the major studios:

> From the late 1920s until the 1960s story conferences were established to develop and control the script. These conferences offered constant feedback to the screenwriter, delivered new ideas, involved crucial decisions, and were therefore seen as an essential part of screenwriting itself. [...] it can be concluded that attending screenwriting conferences accounted for a large amount of the working hours of producers.
>
> (Tieber 2014, 227)

But for a project to even reach the conferencing stage, there first had to be an idea, whether a script, a 'pitch', or an existing literary property, available to adapt. The studios, and even independent production companies, had what were known as story departments staffed by a head of department, a story editor, a range of executive and associate assistants, and readers. The story department would conduct 'intensive searches for new story properties' (Anon. 1941, 34A), whether reviewing stage plays on Broadway or other theatres around the USA, surveying the literary market for bestsellers and other novels, or even reading unsolicited scripts from independent producers and production companies or amateur writers. Reader reports would be written about potential story material to judge its suitability as a production, the potential cost, the potential market, and of course any potential censorship issues. The story department was, in effect, a filter for all of the potential creative ideas that could be made into a feature film.

Outside of the major studios were the 'poverty row' studios: independent producers of low-budget B-movies, such as westerns, horrors, melodramas, and even sexploitation films. They were not studios, but small production outfits, or even just an independent producer. They had no studio lot, but would instead rent studio space from the major studios or even shoot on location. The principal aim of the poverty row studios was to shoot quickly and cheaply. This also meant that poverty row studios were on the constant lookout for cheap story material, often original scripts written by, as one profile piece in the *New York Times* put it,

> any one of the dozen or two writers who earn their livelihood from this type of picture. [...] Sometimes a yarn may be purchased from a little-known pulp writer yearning for the fabulous cinema opportunity for as little as $25.
>
> (Hanna 1939, X6)

Given the tight production values of these kinds of films, poverty row producers would typically borrow scenes from a range of original screenplays to form the most easily filmable and least costly film possible: 'Screen plays are written and rewritten many times until they are tight, compact, devoid of all extraneous material and can be handed to the director to be filmed verbatim' (Hanna 1939, X6). These producers were on the constant lookout for scripts, paying between $25 and $100 per script (Harrison 1936, AA3). What this indicates is the level of creativity that underpinned the 'system'—screenplays or ideas generated by 'amateurs', of which we know there have must have been a substantial number given the proliferation of the screenwriting manual (see Chapter 1)—of which, the vast majority would have remained unmade, or at the very least substantially altered from its original form as submitted to an independent producer or major studio story department.

By the late 1940s and through into the 1950s, the major studios were cutting back on story departments (though they did not altogether abolish them), part of a gradual move towards a new form of production. Studios by the 1950s were reducing the exclusive contracts with creative labourers and instead financing independent producers and production companies on a per-film basis. This now placed the initial creative process in the hands of producers and production companies external to the major Hollywood companies. And what began to emerge was a process of overdevelopment, in which producers were developing more projects than could be feasibly produced and released just so they had a project ready to enter production should a major studio take an interest and offer a deal.

There are two important points to consider here. First, a differentiation was being made between 'professional' screenwriters (see Banks 2015; Tieber 2014) and the 'dime a dozen' amateur and semi-amateur writers submitting screenplays to B-movie producers. Industry studies of Hollywood continues to favour the concept of professionalisation, but when it comes to the unmade, a substantial amount of the creative labour was by those screenwriters not even acknowledged or recognised by professional organisations or institutions (the Writers Guild of America, contracts with studios, the PCA, etc.). Second, underpinning the Hollywood system of film production was a repository of unmade and unrealised creativity; from ideas and scripts, to optioned novels and plays, the Hollywood system was built on, and encouraged, the development of ideas and projects that would never get made. Some of this material is now available in archives, but not all of it. However, the PCA records at the Margaret Herrick Library are one such archival collection where it is possible to unearth this unmade creativity. Studios and producers would submit selected material—whether a synopsis, novel, or script—to the PCA for inspection as to its suitability for filming. They would not submit everything, but the material they did submit could be quite extensive: correspondence, scripts, notes, and budgets. What follows is a brief contextualisation of the PCA.

The Production Code Administration

The PCA was established by the Motion Picture Producers and Distributors of America (MPPDA); the MPPDA (precursor to the Motion Picture Association of America [MPAA]) was Hollywood's trade organisation that promoted and lobbied on behalf of its members—Hollywood's major studios and producers—both within the USA and around the world. The MPPDA was headed by the former Postmaster General of the USA, General Will Hays, who introduced what was informally known as 'the formula' in 1924, a set of moral conventions for film production that producers were advised to follow; most did not (Koszarski 1990, 206–209). The PCA was formed in 1934 in order to implement and enforce the Production Code, a document that was devised by both industry figures and 'moral reformers' in 1930 and acted as a set of guidelines as to what was, and more importantly what was not, acceptable for on-screen representation (Greene 2010, 55). It was part of a wider exercise to 'clean up' the image of Hollywood and of the films produced, acting as a form of self-regulation to avoid any kind of government intervention (Olasky 1984). Prior to the existence of the PCA, compliance with the Code was entirely voluntary. However, following the creation of the PCA, those studios, producers, and production companies that were members of the MPPDA were required to first submit scripts for approval, followed by the produced film, in order to receive a seal of approval for mainstream distribution. Any violation of the Code could lead to a fine of $25,000 (Black 1989, 167). Those producers that were not members of the MPPDA were not bound by the same process, but the MPPDA still encouraged them to submit scripts and films to the PCA to receive a seal of approval. Estimates suggest that, throughout the existence of the Production Code, 95 percent of all films produced in the USA 'were made with oversight from the PCA' (Piepenburg 2018, 105). It is for this reason that the PCA records contain so much archival material, both of produced and of unproduced films and from both member and non-member companies and producers of the MPPDA.

The Production Code and the PCA were a result of years of pressure being exerted by groups from across the USA, most notably the Catholic Church and the Legion of Decency. The principal aim of the Church was to wage a crusade against Hollywood's output and what was termed by religious leaders as a 'fortress of filth' (Black 1989, 167). The Legion of Decency was a Catholic group that was 'dissatisfied [...] with the moral fiber of the motion pictures', and was dedicated to fighting against the production and exhibition of films it deemed objectionable (Kelly and Ford 1957, 387). But the Catholic Church and the Legion of Decency were not the only moral crusaders pressuring the MPPDA to introduce a formalised Production Code and to enforce it. Others pushing for its implementation included political and industrial groups with their own vested interests, including 'women's groups, civic organisations, municipal and state censorship boards' (Black 1989, 167). Will Hays appeased the growing pressure by forming the PCA and appointing Joseph Breen to oversee the administration's activities.

The PCA and its work presents an immediately obvious structural barrier to film production: censorship and industry self-regulation.

Scholarly output typically references a profile piece published in *Liberty* magazine in 1936 about Joseph Breen, in which Breen was described as having 'more influence in standardizing world thinking than Mussolini, Hitler, or Stalin. And, if we should accept the valuation of this man's own business, possibly more than the Pope' (Breen quoted in Doherty 2007, 7). There is an element of mythmaking in this profile piece that obscures the truth of the work being undertaken by Breen and the PCA. Certainly, the PCA was a structural barrier, a hurdle, for studios and producers to overcome between the 1930s and the 1960s, but there were also wider forces and gatekeepers at play (and which arguably continue to exert influence to this day). For while it was a requirement for members of the MPPDA to seek PCA approval for scripts and films, it was not necessarily the PCA that was responsible for a project remaining unmade. The PCA—and Breen—quite often acted as a stakeholder in the creative process in a bid to ensure successful production. This even involved looking for loopholes in the Production Code, with Breen and his team acutely aware of the financial pressures that producers and production companies faced, particularly when heavily investing resources—both financial and creative—into a particular project. As such, the PCA would certainly at times substantially impact on the shape and structure of a script and the final film. But that is a very different issue to the PCA being the contributing factor to the number of unmade films that exist within the PCA records, or for that matter the hundreds, most likely thousands, of other unmade films that now reside in other archives. There were other structural forces beyond the PCA itself that contributed to the unmade, unseen, and unreleased, whether politicians, trade unions, industry organisations, the military, social prejudices, and ignorance (in particular, the cultural conditions surrounding representation of women and their role on and off screen), the internal processes of studios and their story departments, and even the self-sabotaging efforts of producers themselves. However, the PCA became a means by which these external forces could seek to undermine projects in order to protect their own vested interests. As such, Breen and the PCA were quite often negotiating and navigating structural forces beyond the Production Code, but for which the Production Code served as a catalyst.

The original Production Code was co-written by Martin Quigley (an American publisher and founder of the film trade journal *Exhibitors Herald*) and Daniel Lord (a Jesuit priest), though there were many others who had authorial input into the final document (Doherty 2007, 56). Thomas Doherty has highlighted how the original Production Code is somewhat shrouded in mystery, with no definitive copy of the Code from 1930 held by the Margaret Herrick Library (1999, 347). Doherty set about reconstructing as close as possible the original 1930 Code, triangulating his findings with contemporary trade journal sources. His reasons for doing so were clear, stating that 'The extant versions of the Code vary somewhat in typographical details, layout, word choice, and arrangement of the text. Some omit the philosophical passages or lack a later amendment to the "working principles"' (Doherty 1999, 347). Doherty's published version of the Production Code in *Pre-Code Hollywood* (2009) was largely based on a version from 1937 by Olga J. Martin in *Hollywood's Movie Commandments*: 'As Joseph Breen's former secretary, Martin had access to the most complete, contemporaneous documents consulted by Hollywood's in-house censors' (Doherty 1999, 347–367).

The general principles of the Production Code were based on the distinction between entertainment that could 'Improve the race, or, at least, to recreate and rebuild human beings exhausted with the realities of life' and entertainment that could 'Degrade human beings, or to lower their standards of life and living' (Doherty 1999, 348). These overriding philosophical beliefs of how media operated and its potential (harmful) effects on audiences influenced the overall working principles of the Code, which amounted to ensuring that audiences were not exposed to films that lowered the 'moral standard' of society or were forced to sympathise with evil, sin, crime, and wrongdoing (Doherty 1999, 351). The working principles of the Code, and the screen content and topics that were prohibited and regulated, underwent revisions throughout its existence. In summary, the Code applied the below general categories to the scrutiny of scripts and films seeking PCA approval:

Crime: crimes against the law, murder, methods of crime, brutal killings, illegal drug traffic, use of liquor.

Drinking: depiction of drinking, alcoholism.

Brutality, horror, and gruesomeness: murders, repellent subjects, lack of good taste.

Sex: sex morality, love triangles, adultery, scenes of passion, seduction or rape, sex perversion, white slavery, miscegenation, sex hygiene and venereal diseases, scenes of actual childbirth, children's sex organs.

Vulgarity: low, disgusting, unpleasant subjects.

Obscenity: obscenity in word, gesture, reference, song, joke, or by suggestion.

Profanity: profane or vulgar expressions, with a list of prohibited words of phrases listed in the Production Code.

Costume: complete nudity, undressing scenes, indecent or undue exposure, dancing costumes, and underexposure.

Dancing: suggestive dancing.

Religion: religious ridicule, inaccurate religious depiction.

Nationality: national feelings, respectful use of the Flag.

Locations: locations associated with sin or depravity (i.e. brothels).

Titles: salacious, indecent, or otherwise.[1]

The way these principles were applied varied greatly depending on the contexts of individual scripts, films, producers, studios, studio executives, and those administrators writing the report, or on how the overall plot of a project was perceived. Take the issue of sex. The Code differentiated between representing sex as a means of exciting an audience (arousal) or as being impure (love or sex that is against 'human and divine law') versus 'pure love' (Doherty 1999, 354). The latter was permitted when showing the lawful love between a heterosexual couple (upholding the institution of marriage, for example), but it could not lead to representations of passion or lust (Doherty 1999, 355). The Code was by its very nature contradictory and open to interpretation. The constant process of additions and revisions suggests the difficulty the PCA had in being flexible enough to ensure freedom and diversity for screenwriters and film producers, while also being focused enough to prohibit (or at the very least, discourage) topics and behaviours that were deemed morally reprehensible.

These contradictions, along with the application of the Code, have largely been what has concerned scholarly inquiry into Production Code-era Hollywood. There has been a persistent research narrative focused on censorship and moral standards and the means by which the Production Code impacted and shaped the creative processes of those films that were produced. Take, for example, the work of Jane Greene (2010, 2011), who has explored production trends in comedy in 1930s Hollywood and how the Production Code influenced the development of the screwball comedy. Greene's work thoroughly explores the intersection between regulatory policy and the cultural conditions of production, going so far as to suggest that the Code was responsible for the emergence of the antagonistic screwball romantic couple, with dialogue that crackled with an underlying sexual tension and innuendo.

Research has largely remained focused on how the onscreen action that we do see in Production Code-era films is a substitute for that which the Code did not want audiences to see. Scholars like Greene make use of Production Code records at the Margaret Herrick Library, or reference works that make use of this archival documentation, though mostly with a focus on those films that were produced and the ways in which the PCA responded to them.

Case studies abound of produced films from the Production Code era, looking at how the producers and the film industry interacted with the PCA and/or the Production Code, often leading to the argument that the PCA impacted and influenced production trends and was the key structural barrier to creativity. Case studies include K. R. M. Short's (1991) study of the PCA's intervention in the postproduction of *That Hamilton Woman* (1941); studies of war films produced during World War Two to understand the relationship between the PCA, censorship, and propaganda (Chung 2018; Robertson 2020; Webb 2019); discussions of morality and family audiences (Brown 2013; Worland 1999); Leslie Wilson's (2018) exploration of sexuality and gender in *The Secret Six* (1931); investigations into national identity and the cultural Cold War (Chung and Diffrient 2017; Major 2019); studies of censorship in the screenwriting process (Hirsch 2012; Peirse 2018); explorations of communism and civil rights on film (Ooten 2013); consideration of audiences, stardom, and censorship (Maltby 1986); investigations into production histories of how films overcame the stipulations of the Production Code (Kuhn 2013); and case studies of films that challenged and ultimately undermined the Production Code (Simmons 2005).

These case studies are all insightful and necessary microhistories, revealing the subtleties of personal interactions and of the material and cultural conditions of production. But the vast majority of research makes no use of, nor even acknowledges, the existence of the unproduced PCA records at the Margaret Herrick Library. There is a clear oversight in existing knowledge of how Hollywood studios functioned during the Production Code era and of the processes of unmade creativity that underpinned those films that were produced. By focusing heavily on those films that were produced and the role of the PCA intervening in their production, it can (misre)present a picture of Hollywood as being filled with prurient producers that had to be tamed by the PCA. As Joel Timmer rightly indicates, 'since the late 1980s, film historians have conducted several case studies using Production Code Administration (PCA) files to understand the functioning of the PCA and how it applied the Code' (2011, 29). But this narrative is based on the use of archival records pertaining to the produced, with the unproduced files potentially containing histories of wider structural forces impacting on film production.

One case study of an unmade film using the unproduced PCA records is David Welky's article on *The Forty Days of Musa Dagh*. Welky provides a history of why studios like MGM failed to produce an adaptation of author Franz Werfel's novel *The Forty Days of Musa Dagh* (1933) for close to half a century. Welky's study is a thorough insight into geo-politics and Hollywood's ever-increasing reliance on the international box office. Werfel's novel, which tells the story of the massacre of Armenians by Turkish forces in World War One, was culturally and politically sensitive. But Welky considers the unproduced PCA record pertaining to *The Forty Days of Musa Dagh* in isolation, with no reference to it as being an unmade film or part of a wider shadow history of the unmade existing within the PCA records. There is no mention made even of the fact it is part of a wider category of the unproduced. Instead, the project is presented as an insular case study.

The prevailing history of the PCA is heavily influenced by the likes of Leonard Leff and Jerold Simmons' *The Dame in the Kimono* (2001 [1990]), a book that provides an account of the organisation's existence from 1934 to 1966. It draws upon archival records at the Margaret Herrick Library and other institutions (the Will Hays Papers, for example), commencing with *Dead End* (1937) and ending with *Who's Afraid of Virginia Woolf* (1966). The focus is on the means by which the PCA controlled output and created a film culture that was more family orientated. Similarly, Thomas Doherty's work (2007) focuses on Breen above all else and his role in creating this culture. In contrast, Noel Brown (2013) makes a critical intervention on the dominant history of the PCA:

> I would like to challenge some long-standing presumptions regarding Hollywood cinema during this period, namely (1) that it was the Production Code that forced the major Hollywood studios to re-orientate towards 'family' entertainment; and (2) that all films made under the provisions of the Code, differences in taste notwithstanding, were necessarily 'family' films. The latter misconception, which has been promulgated by various historians of note, is particularly significant in that it views Code-era Hollywood and 'family' entertainment as largely coterminous—as, indeed, it was represented by key figures in the industry.
>
> (Brown 2013, 2)

Brown's intervention indicates that the history of the PCA and of Code-era Hollywood is one that requires further investigation. David Eldridge (2000) makes a similar intervention to Brown, focusing on the CIA and the cultural Cold War to argue that there were other forces beyond the PCA that impacted on Hollywood's film output. Most of the above histories also disguise the process of archival research, in a way that can suggest that the PCA records tell a complete and full narrative of the production processes and cultures of the era. But they don't. What I am suggesting is that current literature does not fully take account of the unproduced category within the PCA records. Instead, prevailing discourse resolves the gaps and absences that are apparent by disguising the process of 'doing history' and archival research and with the majority of research privileging those films that were produced and achieved a seal of approval, or those films that challenged the Production Code and contributed towards its demise.

What follows in the next chapter is a discussion of the PCA records and their existence within the Margaret Herrick Library. The aim is to begin foregrounding the unproduced category and to emphasise the materiality of the archival collection.

Note

1 *A Code to Govern the Making of Motion and Talking Pictures, the Reasons Supporting It, and the Resolution for Uniform Interpretation*, June 13, 1934. Core Collection Pamphlets, Margaret Herrick Library.

Works cited

Anon. 1941. '20th-Fox Builds Up Story Department'. *Boxoffice* 38, no. 21: 34A.

Banks, Miranda. 2015. *The Writers: A History of American Screenwriters and Their Guild.* New Brunswick, NJ: Rutgers University Press.

Black, Gregory D. 1989. 'Hollywood Censored: The Production Code Administration and the Hollywood Film Industry, 1930–1940'. *Film History* 3, no. 3: 167–189.

Bordwell, David, Staiger, Janet, and Thompson, Kristin. 1985. *The Classical Hollywood Cinema: Film Style & Mode of Production to 1960*. New York: Routledge.

Brown, Noel. 2013. '"A New Movie Going Public": 1930s Hollywood and the Emergence of the "Family" Film'. *Historical Journal of Film, Radio and Television* 33, no. 1: 1–23.

Chung, Hye S. 2018. 'Hollywood Diplomacy and *The Purple Heart* (1944): Preserving Wartime Alliances through Film Regulation'. *Historical Journal of Film, Radio and Television* 38, no. 3: 495–515.

Chung, Hye S., and Diffrient, David S. 2017. 'The Omnibus Film as Message Picture: Cold War Politics and the Myth of National Unity in *It's A Big Country* (1951)'. *Historical Journal of Film, Radio and Television* 37, no. 3: 499–516.

Doherty, Thomas. 1999. *Pre-Code Hollywood: Sex, Immorality, and Insurrection in American Cinema, 1930–1934*. New York: Columbia University Press.

———. 2007. *Hollywood's Censor: Joseph I. Breen and the Production Code Administration*. New York: Columbia University Press.

Eldridge, David. 2000. '"Dear Owen": The CIA, Luigi Luraschi and Hollywood, 1953'. *Historical Journal of Film, Radio and Television* 20, no. 2: 149–196.

Greene, Jane M. 2010. 'Hollywood's Production Code and Thirties Romantic Comedy'. *Historical Journal of Film, Radio and Television* 30, no. 1: 55–73.

———. 2011. 'A Proper Dash of Spice: Screwball Comedy and the Production Code'. *Journal of Film and Video* 63, no. 3: 45–63.

Hanna, David. 1939. 'Wealth of the "Indies"'. *New York Times*, April 16, X6.

Harrison, Paul. 1936. 'Many Hollywood Stars of Yesteryear Working Today with the "Quickies"'. *The Washington Post*, June 28, AA3.

Hirsch, Pam. 2012. 'Authorship and Propaganda: Phyllis Bottome and the Making of *The Mortal Storm* (1940)'. *Historical Journal of Film, Radio and Television* 32, no. 1: 57–72.

Kelly, Gerald and Ford, John C. 1957. 'The Legion of Decency'. *Theological Studies* 18, no. 3: 387–433.

Koszarski, Richard. 1990. *An Evening's Entertainment: The Age of the Silent Feature Picture, 1915–1928*. Berkeley: University of California Press.

Kuhn, Annette. 2013. 'VD Propaganda, *Dr. Ehrlich's Magic Bullet* and the Production Code'. *Film History: An International Journal* 25, no. 1–2: 130–137.

Leff, Leonard J., and Simmons, Jerold L. 2001. *The Dame in the Kimono: Hollywood, Censorship, and the Production Code*. Lexington: The University Press of Kentucky.

Major, Patrick. 2019. 'Shooting Rommel: *The Desert Fox* (1951) and Hollywood's Public-Private Diplomacy'. *Historical Journal of Film, Radio and Television* 39, no. 2: 209–232.

Maltby, Richard. 1986. '"Baby Face", or How Joe Breen Made Barbara Stanwyck Atone for Causing the Wall Street Crash'. *Screen* 27, no. 2: 22–46.

Olasky, Marvin N. 1984. 'The Failure of Movie Industry Public Relations, 1921–1934'. *Journal of Popular Film and Television* 12, no. 4: 163–170.

Ooten, Melissa. 2013. 'Censorship in Black and White: *The Burning Cross* (1947), *Band of Angels* (1957) and the Politics of Film Censorship in the American South after World War II'. *Historical Journal of Film, Radio and Television* 33, no. 1: 77–98.

Peirse, Alison. 2018. 'The Script, The Séance and The Censor: Writing *Night of the Demon* (1957)'. *Historical Journal of Film, Radio and Television* 38, no. 1: 73–94.

Piepenburg, Claire. 2018. 'Not Yet Rated: Self-Regulation and Censorship Issues in the U.S. Film Industry'. *UCLA Entertainment Law Review* 25, no. 1: 97–131.

Regev, Ronny. 2016. 'Hollywood Works: How Creativity became Labor in the Studio System'. *Enterprise & Society* 17, no. 3: 591–617.

Robertson, Barry. 2020. '"So Many Brutes and…So Many Decent Guys": Nunally Johnson and the Making of *The Moon is Down* (1943)'. *Historical Journal of Film, Radio and Television* 40, no. 4: 683–701.

Schatz, Thomas. 2010. *The Genius of the System: Hollywood Filmmaking in the Studio Era*. Minneapolis: University of Minnesota Press, [1988].

Short, Kenneth R.M. 1991. '*That Hamilton Woman* (1941): Propaganda, Feminism and the Production Code'. *Historical Journal of Film, Radio and Television* 11, no. 1: 3–19.

Simmons, Jerold. 2005. 'Challenging the Production Code: *The Man with the Golden Arm*'. *Journal of Popular Film and Television* 33, no. 1: 39–48.

Tieber, Claus. 2014. '"A Story Is Not a Story, but a Conference": Story Conferences and the Classical Studio System'. *Journal of Screenwriting* 5, no. 2: 225–237.

Timmer, Joel. 2011. 'Restricting Portrayals of Film Violence to Reduce the Likelihood of Negative Effects in Viewers: Did the Framers of the Motion Picture Production Code Get It Right?' *Journal of Popular Film and Television* 39, no. 1: 29–36.

Webb, Brandon. 2019. '"Hitler Must be Laughed at!" The PCA, Propaganda and the Perils of Parody During Wartime'. *Historical Journal of Film, Radio and Television* 39, no. 4: 749–767.

Wilson, Leslie. 2018. 'Frances Marion, *The Secret Six*, and the Evolving Heroine in 1930s Hollywood'. *Historical Journal of Film, Radio and Television* 38, no. 2: 246–262.

Worland, Rick. 1999. 'The Korean War Film as Family Melodrama: *The Bridges at Toko-Ri* (1954)'. *Historical Journal of Film, Radio and Television* 19, no. 3: 359–377.

3 The Margaret Herrick Library and the PCA records

The Margaret Herrick Library is the repository headquarters of the Academy of Motion Picture Arts and Sciences (AMPAS), located at the Center for Motion Picture Study in Beverly Hills, Los Angeles. AMPAS was founded in 1927 and the Margaret Herrick Library in 1928. The holdings of the Library are extensive, with its special collections ranging from the papers of some of Hollywood's most famous directors (Alfred Hitchcock, Mary Pickford), producers (Samuel Goldwyn, Irving Thalberg), and actors (Gregory Peck, Katharine Hepburn, et al.), to manuscript collections of entire studios (the MGM collection, for example, contains over '40,000 script items documenting 1900 productions from 1918 to 1986') (Mehr 1996, 22). As described by Linda Harris Mehr, the Library's holdings, which continue to expand, document film as 'both an art form and an industry. [It is] one of the world's most extensive and comprehensive research and reference collections' (1996, 19). The scope of archival material held at the Margaret Herrick Library is overwhelming and has been central to the research agenda of film and media historians for many decades. While not the only major archive documenting Hollywood and the American film industry, it is certainly one of the most important.

The archive can be accessed both physically (visiting the Library) and digitally (parts of the collections have been digitised and made available online). But given its size, where does one even begin? What are the considerations needed to commence research? And how does one find the requisite information and data required in the process of 'doing history'? What I want to first discuss is the (perhaps obvious) means of conducting archival research. This will be a process that is familiar to academics and researchers alike. The point of discussing it here, however, is to foreground the quite often challenging nature of trying to locate the unmade within the archive.

DOI: 10.4324/9781003206118-3

There are two main routes to negotiating the Margaret Herrick Library. The first is to build a working relationship with the librarians and archival staff and to draw upon their own knowledge, expertise, and navigational experience of the archive. And the second is the archive catalogue, available online (https://collections.new.oscars.org/search/advanced). From my own experience of using archive catalogues, I first proceed to browse the collections with no particular aims or objectives in mind. I do this in order to get a sense of the way material is catalogued and the kinds of collections an archive holds. Rather than using limited search terms in the first instance (limited in the sense that the search will narrow in on particular metadata, potentially at the exclusion of relevant material), this process of browsing helps me to build up an understanding and 'feel' for an archive, as well as the means by which it has been catalogued. And it relates to a third alternative route of archival negotiation, which comprises contingency, experience, and information.

Browsing an archival catalogue at the top level (i.e. collections) might arouse curiosity for a particular archival holding you were not aware existed. We can take the Alan J. Pakula Papers as a random example. The catalogue's hierarchy browser breaks down the collection by subcollection, subseries, and ultimately the archival record. Each click reveals yet another layer of categorisation, with ever new depths and layers to what the papers contain and how they have been organised, eventually leading to a category relating to the unmade:

> Collections—Alan J. Pakula Papers—Manuscripts Subcollection—Production Files—Unproduced Subseries

Clicking on the 'Unproduced Subseries' reveals an abundance of records that seem to scroll on endlessly down the page. In fact, the 'Unproduced Subseries' runs from file 831 (*Abraham*) to file 1181 (*The Wolves of Willoughby Chase*), with a whole swathe of unproduced projects listed: *The Martian Chronicles*, *The Intimate Diary of a Russian Woman*, *The Mummy Market*, *St. Ubain's Horseman*, *The Secret History*, and many others. The point here is about how it is quite often necessary to look beyond what the repository advertises as its main holdings. For example, the former director of the Library, Linda Harris Mehr, makes no reference to the unmade in her account of the Margaret Herrick Library's holdings. Indeed, Mehr's account makes it clear that the Library has an extensive collection of screenplays for 'produced films' (Mehr 1996, 21). But what of the unproduced? Once again, it is as if such material does not exist.

There is a category within the Margaret Herrick Library catalogue for 'Unproduced Scripts', with the scope of material ranging from 1956 to 1996. The collection is 'artificial' in the sense that it was created by archivists out of pre-existing material that was held by the Library (in contrast to archival provenance, in which collections are deposited with an institution and, by and large, preserved in the order in which they are received). As the summary states, 'The artificial collection created by the Library contains nearly 100 unproduced story properties. In most cases there is one file per film title and the file contains only one script' (Unproduced Scripts n.d.). But herein lies the problem: while it is noteworthy that the Margaret Herrick Library has acknowledged the existence of the unmade within its repository, it is trying to easily categorise, and thereby resolve, the inherent gaps and absences that the unmade presents. It is material that defies such easy categorisation. And at the same time, the Library has pre-designated that to be classed as unproduced, a script must be in existence. Of the unmade files I have mentioned above from the Alan J. Pakula Papers, none are linked to the 'Unproduced Scripts' collection.

To further complicate this, if I use the search function of the online Margaret Herrick Library catalogue, using the keyword 'unproduced' (the term used by the Library) and searching the Library holdings, it returns just 2,850 records, and when I search within those records, again the files listed above in the Alan J. Pakula Papers are not part of the search results. If I search for the unproduced in the collections category, it returns only three results: 'Paramount Pictures unproduced story property synopses 1949', 'Unproduced Scripts 1956–1996', and 'Zake Steiner collection of unproduced scripts 1984'. In short, the unmade is hidden, scattered across collections, buried within subseries, and often overlooked as even being unmade, unproduced, lost, creative debris, or whatever other way you want to label it. Attempts have been made to resolve this problematic material through artificial means, as noted above, but in doing so it has further marginalised the extent of material that exists.

The above process is largely how I came to understand the unmade within the Margaret Herrick Library, including within the Production Code Administration (PCA) records. The PCA records document the activities of the PCA and its interactions with producers, studios, screenwriters, industry representatives, politicians, and other lobbying parties. Exact estimates of the number of projects housed in the PCA records are around 20,000 (the public facing catalogue states 'more than 19,500', while reference librarians suggest more than 20,000) (Genevieve Maxwell, email message to author, June 9, 2020). It is probably more useful to consider the PCA records in terms of measurement, totalling 240 linear feet of papers. These records pertain to individual film properties submitted to the PCA for approval or, more often than not, analysis as to their suitability against the Production Code. Each of the records contain many documents, primarily correspondence, but usually accompanying creative material as well, usually consisting of a treatment or a novel proposed for adaptation in the first instance. The summary description in the Margaret Herrick Library catalogue provides the following detail:

> The files contain clippings, including film reviews and other articles; correspondence, including interoffice memos and memos 'to the files'; analysis charts; synopses; credit sheets; theater and book reviews; and censor board reports. Some files may include script excerpts, treatments, music and lyrics, meeting notes, and in rare instances, photographs.
>
> (Production Code Administration Records, n.d.)

The description makes it clear that the records contain an assortment of historical information, much of which may not have been directly generated by the staff at the PCA, but gathered from external bodies. The records span 1927 to 1967 inclusive, meaning that they incorporate historical evidence that precedes the introduction of the Production Code by three years and the formation of the PCA by seven years. They contain the original Production Code pamphlets, annual reports, and production files from between 1930 and 1968.[1] These documents trace the evolution of the Production Code, reflecting changing social mores or the attitudes of the incumbent PCA administrator, as well as the production trends within Hollywood as perceived by the PCA and the scripts submitted to it.

The annual PCA reports hint at the scale of the unmade across the history of Hollywood. They list statistics of projects submitted to the PCA (both films and scripts), as well as titles submitted for registration to the Motion Picture Association of America (MPAA) Title Registration Bureau.[2] When looking at these statistics, purely at the surface level, it becomes clear that there is a disparity between the existing history of produced films and the abundance of those films that remained unmade. For example, according to a 1952 annual report, between 1938 and 1952 there were an estimated 53,983 titles registered with the Bureau, 8,600 original stories and adaptations approved for production between 1935 and 1952, but only 5,345 feature films released by member companies of the MPAA between 1935 and 1952

Table 3.1 MPAA PCA records manuscript subcollection series

A—Broken Blossoms	Broken Journey—Diamond Queen
Diamond Safari—Girls of the Road	Girls of the Sierra—Iron Glove
Iron Horse—Magnificent Seven	Magnificent Tramp—Old Maid
Old Man—Romance of the West	Romance on the High Seas—Stubborn Wood
Student Prince—Valley of the Vengeance	Valley of Wanted Men—Z
Additions received 1989	Card files

(excluding re-issues).[3] When including feature-length films released by non-member companies of the MPAA, the figure increases to 7,967. Of course, this is based on estimates by the PCA. But it does suggest a discrepancy between the produced and the unproduced with this only being data based on that material or those films *approved* by the PCA. It indicates that even when a project was approved by the PCA, it was not necessarily guaranteed to go into production.

The privileging of the produced within the PCA records is clear by how the catalogue hierarchy browser does not differentiate between the produced and the unproduced. The manuscripts subcollection is ordered alphabetically by project title (see Table 3.1). So in order to locate the unproduced within the PCA records, it is necessary to rely on the metadata input by the Library's archivists.

The primary process of locating the unproduced is via the Library's advanced search function. Using the keyword of 'unproduced', setting the collections to 'Motion Picture Association of America. Production Code Administration records', and the data set to 'Library Holdings', this returns 911 records that contain the word 'unproduced' in the metadata, under half of the estimated figure (according to archival staff) of how many files in the PCA records actually pertain to the unproduced.

For the purposes of this case study, conducted during the coronavirus pandemic of 2020–2021, I am going to focus on the digitally available PCA records. Around 2,000 of the PCA records have been digitised, with 1,000 of these available online publicly via the Margaret Herrick Library Digital Collections. Using the same search principles as above, it is possible to identify 38 records digitally available that contain 'unproduced' in the metadata (see Appendix I). This equates to roughly 4 percent of the digital records available being classed as unproduced, which, when extrapolated to the identified 911 out of the 20,000 (around 4.5 percent) in the main collection, is an approximate equivalent sample range. Of the 38 records identified, 6 of the records contain documentation that precedes the formation of the PCA in 1934 or the introduction of the Production Code in 1930.

In analysing these records, I am not—in the first instance anyway—looking beyond their archival existence to understand anything else about them. The unmade and the archive are inextricably linked and the methods of the unproduction studies scholar is to understand the material evidence as being, first and foremost, tied to the conditions of the archival institution. As such, I want to consider them in their material (albeit digital) form within the PCA records. Whether any of the projects were later produced is irrelevant (for this study) to the archival material in the form in which it exists in the Margaret Herrick Library. But if the files do mention previous adaptations—for example, the *Coquette* file makes reference to an earlier screen adaptation by Mary Pickford—that is relevant information in the context of the material in the archive. The aim here is to highlight the potential methods of unproduction studies and to foreground the gaps and absences in the frustrating process of archival research.

Instead, I am suggesting that a means of progressing within unproduction studies is to move beyond subsuming individual records, or individual documents, into existing canonical, dominant histories, thereby once more contributing to the career surveys of 'successful' filmmakers and attempting to resolve the absences in knowledge. Such an approach continues the process of marginalisation of forgotten histories and the privileging of the produced, i.e. that in order to understand the unmade it has to be explicitly linked *to* the produced. Rather, the archive can be seen as a contested site of this marginalised and forgotten history and that the gaps and absences should actually be confronted. Unproduction studies has the potential to emphasise the archival process and the materiality of the archive, as discussed in Chapter 1. So the reason for taking the approach that I do in this case study is to highlight the unstable nature of the object of study being examined. The PCA records do not provide a linear, consistent narrative, with all correspondence, creative material, and conversations in a complete form recorded for posterity.

Take, for example, how in the *Circus Parade* file, made up of twenty-seven separate documents, there is what appears to be a random letter that does not seem to relate in any way to the surrounding material. It is a letter about someone called Mrs. Northrup of Portland, Oregon. Someone (it is not clear who) has written to Jason Joy, of the Motion Picture Producers and Distributors of America (MPPDA), to request that Mrs. Northrup be affiliated with the organisation, 'in a similar capacity to that of Mrs. Winter'.[4] Mrs. Northrup is mentioned nowhere else in the file and the entire context of the letter is insular. What does it mean? Why is it in the *Circus Parade* file? Is it a vital clue? Or is it just a misfiled letter retained in the original filing order of the PCA records? There are other examples like this. And there are other documents that are indecipherable. This is particularly the case with handwritten documents, or documents with handwritten notations. These items often convey personal insights but are incredibly difficult to accurately interpret. Most frustrating are the scraps of paper with doodles and other notes scrawled on them, as in the example of one such piece of evidence in the *Spy Ships* file. At the bottom of this scrap of paper, it clearly reads, 'Attach this to our file [...] *Navy Spy*'.[5] To the left of this are a series of random numbers, some with illegible writing next to them, and at the top of the page are a couple of sentences that I am unable to make out. What does it mean and how is one meant to make sense of it? Given the request to 'attach this to our file', surely it must mean something, but I am unable to comprehend what exactly.

The unmade is a shadow history precisely because it is composed of material that has been forgotten and so can usually only be understood on its own terms within the archive. It cannot be a part of the canonical history because it is a separate counter history told through the materiality of the archive, while its very materiality means it cannot be easily subsumed because of the incomplete nature of what is being studied.

Analysing the records

To understand the 38 unproduced PCA records that I have identified for this case study, and the material that they contain, I have mapped the documentation within them, extracting key dates, names, production companies, and document type (correspondence, treatments, memo for the files, etc.). I have also analysed each record in order to identify the genre of the story being considered for production, and whether it was an original story, an adaptation, or a remake. The results of this mapping exercise are detailed in Appendix I. I have not included details about the reasons for why the projects were left unmade as this is not always possible to ascertain. Conducting the mapping exercise highlights apparent discrepancies between the catalogue metadata and the actual archival records. Regularly, the metadata in the Margaret Herrick Library ascribes just one production company or studio as being affiliated to the individual record. However, quite often there are multiple production companies or studios affiliated with the record at some point, as detailed in correspondence or creative material submitted to the PCA.

The discrepancy in metadata can be misleading, as in the example of the record for *Child Bride*. The metadata implies that the file contains material only from 1938 and ascribes Columbia as the sole affiliated studio. However, within the forty-two pages of documentation, there is no obviously dated material from 1938, with the material dated either 1943 or 1948. Nor does any of the material contain any information clearly ascribing the project to Columbia. Instead, the project is a film produced by Raymond Friedgen, who is working with the distributor Astor Pictures. The only mention of Columbia is on an undated page, what is possibly an interoffice PCA memo or report, headed 'On the subject of *Child Wives* or *Child Marriage—Child Bride*'.[6] The document lists three projects related to the theme of child marriage, including a 1938 project being developed by Columbia titled *Child Bride* that was abandoned. The *Child Bride* record is an anomaly within the 38 records, for while it is labelled as being unproduced, the bulk of the correspondence pertains to an independent, exploitation film produced by Friedgen and which had been distributed in parts of the USA without a PCA seal of approval. It is the one record that is about a film that definitely existed and is, therefore, mostly likely incorrectly labelled as unproduced.

The majority of the documentation within the 38 records is made up of correspondence, either between film producers and the PCA or between film producers and other external agencies. And the issue of archival and historical absences becomes clear when considering the availability of creative material. Only 24 of the 38 records contain any creative material directly submitted to the PCA (synopsis, treatment, outline, etc.). Of those, only 6 records contain a PCA reader's report: a short one-page summary, written by PCA administrators, of a script or novel that had been submitted for approval. Usually the reader's reports contain a short synopsis, around a paragraph in length, with the remainder of the report focused on issues of problems in the narrative and the suitability or otherwise when judged against the Production Code.

The lack of available creative material is not uncommon in unproduction studies. It highlights not only the fact that unproduction studies is dealing with gaps in historical knowledge, but also how there is a difficulty in ascertaining wider contexts of a project or even a genre for the project. In contrast to the 'Unproduced Collections' of the Margaret Herrick Library, which specifies scripts as being what constitutes worthiness for inclusion in the collection, the unproduced files of the PCA records are largely composed of documents that are evidence of human-to-human interaction about creative material that is no longer available, or at least not available in this particular archive. But even with limited access to creative material there are other ways to obtain information about the proposed projects, usually from the correspondence between the producers and the PCA. Take, for example, *Those Who Trespass*, a record that contains only two documents, totalling four pages of information. The first is a letter sent by John W. Arent (Laurel Films Inc.) to Joseph Breen, dated August 28, 1950. Arent's letter is a standard submission letter to the PCA, common across all of the records:

> I am attaching hereto copy of script on "THOSE WHO TRESPASS". We would greatly appreciate it if you would have someone go over this and advise us as quickly as possible regarding its conformity to the production code requirements.[7]

On the surface, this letter is hardly remarkable, merely a request for approval from a production company to the PCA. But in the context of the 38 records as a whole, it does show how, even without the availability of creative material, it is possible to gain a sense of the creative project being considered. In this case, it is clear the Arent had submitted a fully formed script to the PCA. More typically across the 38 files, producers would submit only a novel or a brief outline in the first instance. This was particularly the case with major studios: MGM, Warner Bros., Paramount, etc. There is also a tone of urgency in the letter, with Arent requesting that the PCA respond as 'quickly as possible'. Presumably, Arent's urgency was a result of a resource implication, with Laurel Films most likely having limited finances to commit to a particular project. Finally, it is possible to detect the potential genre of the script. Arent reveals the title—*Those Who Trespass*—which implies a potential element of crime through the use of the word 'trespass'. It is important to locate evidence of references to potential titles because the title ascribed to the project in the metadata is not always accurate and because many projects would undergo regular title changes throughout the development process. So, in summary, what at first appears to be a seemingly trivial letter is in fact a vital source of information to the unproduction studies scholar.

Still, the letter from Laurel Films does not provide enough information to confirm what the story of *Those Who Trespass* is about. The second document in the record is a three-page response from Joseph Breen to John Arent, sent nine days after the initial submission. Breen's reply is again fairly common across the 38 records. In this instance, Breen writes that *Those Who Trespass* is 'basically acceptable'—one of several stock phrases and sentences that Breen uses—but provides a list of recommendations of revisions to be made to the script before production commences.[8] It is possible to understand what kind of film was being proposed through these recommendations. Breen's word choices in his response include 'revenge motif', 'divorce', 'the beating up [...] seems excessively brutal and gruesome', 'raped', 'Bob beats Caroline', 'beating of a woman', 'throw up and spoil your rug', 'Vinnie's expression, "get even"', 'breasts of women'.[9] Taken together, these word choices allow for an estimation of the kind of story being developed. A crime of passion, maybe? A story of adultery, even? However, these are the only available clues within the record about the creative focus of *Those Who Trespass*.

One final point about this particular record is the lack of any clear evidence of why it has been classed as unproduced. Again, this lack of information is not uncommon across the 38 records (or across archival remains of the unmade generally). The PCA was happy for the *Those Who Trespass* script to proceed into production—Breen's 'basically acceptable' remark indicates this—though with a seal of approval being subject to the final judgement of the finished picture. There is no indication that the PCA was the barrier to the film's unproduced status in this instance, at least based on the available archival evidence. It must be noted, however, that Breen's letter makes it clear that the script had been submitted to the PCA at some point in the past, at which point it had been rejected. Presumably, revisions would have been made to the script that led to its confident resubmission by John Arent. But with no material evidence that the PCA was the barrier, nor any indication of why *Those Who Trespass* was left unmade, what remains are two documents that represent the absence of historical context or information, a clear gap in knowledge and understanding, and a material record of the shadow history of the unmade. The two documents also signify the considerable effort, creative and administrative labour, and financial investment by both the producers (Laurel Films, which would have hired someone, maybe more than one person, to write and rewrite the script) and the PCA (which had its administrators read the script at least twice). So while it might not be possible to understand what *Those Who Trespass* was about (beyond reasonable estimation based on material evidence) or why it failed, it is possible to say that the record indicates the level of resources within Hollywood invested in the unmade.

There are two potential reasons for the lack of creative material within the 38 records. The first is that producers and production companies across the sample repeatedly request that the PCA return scripts or treatments so that they can be submitted to various studios and other production companies in a bid to raise production financing. The records show that the producers were, in effect, shopping the projects around Hollywood, which is why many of the records contain references to numerous studios and production companies. The film projects either were being sent to multiple companies in one year by the same producer or had multiple 'lives' with phases of development across months, years, or even decades, during which time the project would be picked up and then dropped again by different producers and companies. The second reason is that producers and studios resisted committing resources to developing a full script, or even an extended treatment, for the fear of failure. Instead, the records indicate that producers were inclined to submit to the PCA nothing but a brief synopsis of an original story or, quite often, a novel or stage play for adaptation. This was a speculative process in which producers were attempting to gauge the level of problems that might be encountered in developing a project and the resources that might be required to successfully produce it. The unproduced records therefore imply that the entire process of development in Hollywood was predicated on the logic and anticipation of a project more likely remaining unmade. Indeed, it could well be that the preponderance for adaptations of existing literary material within these 38 files was because it limited the resource commitment required by studios and production companies: adapting a novel was a safe option that mitigated financial risk.

*

The mapping of the 38 unproduced PCA records allows for the material conditions of production to be emphasised, i.e. the form in which the records now exist and the way in which they can be understood as being unmade. But the mapping exercise also brings to the fore the wider structural forces at work that contributed to the projects remaining unmade. Rather than the PCA being the only structural barrier to success in the period between the 1930s and 1960s, it was instead one organisation that was part of a wider complex network of negotiation, struggle, and invested interests often beyond its control. What follows in the succeeding chapters is an analysis of key themes that emerge from the 38 records, an exploration of the structural barriers that contributed to the unmade, and an assessment of how the records can contribute to a wider history of unmade Hollywood.

Notes

1 The Production Code pamphlets and the PCA annual reports are available digitally at the following web address: http://digitalcollections.oscars.org/cdm/search/collection/p15759coll11/searchterm/C0D34R/order/date.
2 The MPAA Title Registration Bureau was introduced in 1925 as a means of regulating the ownership of potential feature film titles; member companies would often submit hundreds of titles in a bid to ensure exclusive use, even if there was never any intention to use the title for a production. Archive records exist of reams of paper filled with variations of a particular film title. The system greatly favoured the major studios over independent studios, as the Society of Independent Motion Picture Producers argued in the 1940s.
3 Annual Report of the Motion Picture Association of America, 1952, PAM 759 (1952), PCA Records, The Margaret Herrick Library Digital Collection (MHLDC).
4 Letter from Jason Joy to Charlie C. Pettijohn, October 28, 1929, *Circus Parade*, PCA records, MHLDC.
5 Notation. n.d., *Spy Ships*, PCA records, MHLDC.
6 On the subject of *Child* Wives. n.d. *Child Bride*, PCA records, MHLDC.
7 Letter from John W. Arent to Joseph Breen, August 28, 1950, *Those Who Trespass*, PCA records, MHLDC.
8 Letter from Joseph Breen to John Arent, September 6, 1950, *Those Who Trespass*, PCA records, MHLDC.
9 Ibid.

Works cited

Mehr, Linda H. 1996. 'Center for Motion Picture Study. The Margaret Herrick Library and the Academy Film Archive'. *Historical Journal of Film, Radio and Television* 16, no. 1: 19–25.

Production Code Administration Records. n.d. Academy of Motion Picture Arts and Sciences. https://collections.new.oscars.org/Details/Collection/627.

Unproduced Scripts. n.d. Academy of Motion Picture Arts and Sciences. https://collections.new.oscars.org/Details/Collection/648.

4 Women

There is an absence of women in the 38 Production Code Administration (PCA) records and those women that are either referred to or involved in correspondence are subject to patriarchal attitudes and behaviour. A key example of gender being imposed as a structural barrier to success is *All Flags Flying*. The project was a proposed film adaptation of a stage play written by Edna Riley. The *All Flags Flying* project, along with others in the PCA records, hints at a history of women being subjugated by men in Hollywood, both as creative labourers and in the way they were represented in films that were produced. Indeed, the fate of *All Flags Flying*, and other projects like it (*Case History*, discussed below), rested on the verdict of men who, in the available archival documentation, display predisposing sexist attitudes. The focus of the analysis in this chapter is on how men aimed to control women and the representation of the female body, commencing with a consideration of the *All Flags Flying* file. The chapter also demonstrates how the topic of rape was a recurring theme of unmade projects in the 1940s and 1950s across the sample of PCA records.

*

The *All the Flags* flying file contains no creative material. It comprises correspondence, a memo, two news clippings, and two PCA readers' reports that provide summaries of Edna Riley's stage play. The play is set during World War One, with the action split between domestic scenes in New Jersey and wartime scenes in France. It tells the story of an illicit affair and the secret of an illegitimate child. The archival documentation spans September 1934 through to the spring of 1935 and indicates that Riley was attempting to sell the play to multiple major Hollywood studios for adaptation. The challenge Riley faced in securing interest in the play was considerable, as she herself acknowledged

DOI: 10.4324/9781003206118-4

in a letter she wrote to Cardinal Hayes, of the Legion of Decency, in 1934. Riley told Hayes that she had submitted her play to an open call for material put out by Twentieth Century Pictures and that it was only one of two plays selected from a 'deluge of manuscripts', with 'over a 1000 plays' submitted in response to the call.[1] Her agent had also submitted the play to Paramount for consideration. Both studios had expressed an interest in the play, but had stopped short of committing to it until the PCA had approved the basic story.

So far, the *All Flags Flying* files do not reveal anything that is unusual in the PCA process. However, Riley's letter to Hayes was a letter of protest against the fact that the play had not been approved by the PCA. Joseph Breen claimed that the PCA had never received the play, had no knowledge of what it was about, and had not been consulted by either of the two studios interested in it.[2] As such, Breen made enquiries to the relevant story departments of the studios, with both studios confirming that they had briefly considered the play for adaptation, but internal processes had led to 'any thought of it being adapted for the screen' being abandoned.[3] The files show that the PCA was not the barrier that had led to *All Flags Flying* being left unproduced in the first instance, but internal forces within Paramount and Twentieth Century Pictures. What those processes were is unclear, with a gap in documentation in the PCA files. Yet, this clearly shows how studios themselves were often responsible for leaving projects unmade before even offering them up for verdict by the PCA. This indicates how further archival research into the respective internal policies and procedures of major Hollywood studios is required.

However, Edna Riley herself seems to have caused consternation amongst men at the PCA and the Legion of Decency. This was arguably as a result of Riley's confident determination to get her play adapted, which in turn led to a hardened resistance to *All Flags Flying* amongst the men concerned. Joseph Breen is the first to display a condescending attitude towards Riley in the files, an attitude that is not on display in other files when dealing with combative men (see below for the discussion on *Spy Ships* and Chapter 6 for the discussion of *Circus Parade*). He tells Will Hays that 'the lady' needs to be informed of her 'complete error' and that the Catholic Church appointed him to his role at the PCA; Breen was referring to a remark made by Riley in her letter to Cardinal Hayes.[4]

After this initial bout of correspondence, the PCA invited Paramount to informally submit Riley's play in order to obtain a report on its suitability judged against the Production Code. But in a report on the play by the PCA's Karl Lischka, Riley's gender is once again brought up: 'We are assured by the writer (a woman—God help us!) that this is an unemasculated tale, told with intelligence and dignity. I, for one, am unable to discover point or punch, sense or substance in it'.[5] Lischka took issue with the way Riley represented women in her play, not necessarily how it complied with the Production Code, writing:

> Woman is naturally and normally monogamous. A woman can sin with her lover and, even although violating chastity, still be chaste. Promiscuity, however, at once means prostitution. While a man may fancy himself to like two women at the same time sufficiently to desire to possess both, a good woman cannot do so—it is psychologically impossible for her. Call it the double standard if you will. After all, the so-called double standard is based on sound rational psychology as well as on the immemorial experience of civilized mankind.[6]

It was on the basis of Lischka's report, and his assertion of the story's error in representing female psychology, that Joseph Breen recommended Paramount should not purchase the play, though this was a decision the studio had already made prior to the PCA's report.[7] The final document in the *All Flags Flying* file is a copy of two news clippings that indicate the PCA was keeping abreast of Riley's reactions to the way the industry had responded to her play. In the spring of 1935, she staged a protest outside the offices of the Legion of Decency in New York. Ultimately, however, Riley's efforts to convince the industry of the legitimacy of her play were futile and it remained unmade. The material evidence in the *All Flags Flying* files broadly suggests that both Riley and her play were viewed as a threat by major studios (Paramount, Twentieth Century Pictures) and the PCA because of the fact that she was a woman writing about women.

Such cultural and social value judgements about women are also present in a number of other PCA records, including *Burning Secret*, *Case History*, *Congai*, *Coquette*, *House of Mist*, *Lysistrata*, *Ships in the River*, *The Weather in the Streets*, and *There's One in Every Town*. Most of the evidence in the files indicates that each of the stories was about social themes and society's ills, with one clear recurring topic: rape. Male producers were keen to represent rape on screen, though with differing motives. For some, it was clear exploitation, while for others it was a desire (however problematic) to instigate a broader societal discussion about women's experiences of rape and sexual abuse. *Case History* is a clear example of both of these approaches, given the multiple attempts by different producers to produce the film.

Case History is one of the more complete files within the 38 PCA records, containing 14 individual documents totalling 75 pages of documentation. It is also more complete in the fact that it contains three outlines of seven pages each (though one of these is a duplicate) and one treatment of thirty pages. The project was an intended remake of a Swedish film, and referred to in the files with varying titles: *The Case of Ingegerd Bremssen*, *The Case of Ingrid Bremsen*, *The Scar*, and *Case History*. The project was originally being pursued by Columbia's Harry Cohn and producer William Dozier in September 1950. The first version of the story, titled *The Scar*, is about a woman who, in the weeks leading up to her wedding, is raped by a stranger. Her father, not wanting to attract adverse publicity, urges her not to talk about the crime, against the advice of the doctor that treats her. The doctor warns that keeping quiet will lead to irrevocable psychological damage as well as allow the perpetrator to escape. As the doctor explains, 'Ninety-five percent of all cases are unreported for obvious reasons. Though it is understandable, it creates a serious situation. This action ties the hands of the police and thus increases the incident of the crime'.[8] Over time the woman becomes increasingly anxious as she keeps reliving the rape in her mind. She eventually confides in her fiancé, but he refuses to believe her story: 'He chooses rather to believe that she is not all she pretends to be. Perhaps, he hints, she is not as inexperienced as she would have him believe. These accusations stun her'.[9] The woman notices a local news story about a man standing trial for an undisclosed crime—it's the man that raped her. She decides to attend the trial in a bid to confront her attacker. However, after the man is acquitted of the crime he is being tried for, the woman follows him and kills him with a gun she has found, before handing herself to the authorities. The final act of the story focuses on the woman's murder trial. She is ultimately acquitted when she confesses that she killed the man because he raped her, and with her confession 'her sense of deep shame and degradation begins to fade'.[10]

The Scar is an exploration of the psychological impact of rape on women and the way society (and men) treat rape and rape victims, focusing on the issue of silence. The story makes the case for society as a whole to listen to the voices of women and their experiences of rape. But the PCA rejected the story on the grounds that the woman commits a premeditated murder of the rapist and because the rapist was portrayed as a 'sex pervert'.[11] In this instance, it was the PCA responsible for the film remaining unmade, but the same prevailing attitudes that were observed in the *All Flags Flying* files are on display in the *Case History* files too, suggesting that structural sexism across the film industry was a far wider problem than just the PCA. In his letter to Columbia's B. B. Kahane, Joseph Breen wrote, 'The subject matter is, we think, thoroughly distasteful, and is the kind of material which gives serious offense to great numbers of people in all parts of the world'.[12] But Breen's reasoning in the letter is not in reference to the Production Code, but rather to wider industrial trends and perceived social and cultural attitudes. The PCA's belief that *The Scar* was inappropriate for film production was due to the organisation's experience with a film called *Outrage* (1950), which had received a seal of approval. *Outrage* partially dealt with the subject matter of rape, but, as Breen notes, the public reaction was 'very definitely unfavorable and we have come in for a great deal of severe criticism because of it'.[13] Breen's latter remark to Kahane hints that the reason *The Scar* cannot be approved by the PCA is not because of the Production Code, but rather because of the cultural conditions in the USA. *The Scar* was rejected out of a process of risk mitigation and brand management, with Breen looking to protect the reputation of the PCA in the face of wider cultural attitudes towards women.

The archival documents show that Columbia decided to engage in a process of story revision in a bid to win the PCA's approval. It is likely, given that the PCA had not explicitly rejected *The Scar* on the basis of story content, but rather with reference to wider industrial trends and the reputational risk to the organisation, the producers envisaged they could circumvent any anxieties that Breen had by engaging with him on a creative basis. What follows in the *Case History* files are a series of letters and memos reflecting this creative engagement between the PCA and Columbia. The process begins with Columbia's William Dozier responding to Breen in a letter in which he explains the studio's motives. Columbia's aim was not to produce a film that was in bad taste, but rather to present something different:

> In the present struggle for pictures which are 'different', and which have some ingredient upon which to base a hope for commercial success (without which we shall all soon be out of business), I feel we must strive to bring within the bounds of good taste what might otherwise appear to be a tasteless and objectionable subject. My interest in this particular story goes back about a year and a half, at which time I intended to make it with Miss Fontaine. I mention this only so you will know I have not latched onto it, nor has it been handed to me, as an ill-conceived or impulsively arrived at bit of sensationalism.[14]

Dozier's case for approving *The Scar* was one based on commercial imperatives—i.e. that audiences wanted something 'different'—somewhat in contrast to Breen's claims that audiences had responded 'unfavourably' to similar films in the past. Dozier's letter even challenges the notion of 'taste', perhaps recognising that a structural barrier exists in regard to cultural attitudes towards women and rape, but looking to be the first producer to challenge and break down such a barrier. Dozzier planned to revise the story in order to ensure that it avoided any conflict with the Production Code (i.e. altering the way the girl murders the rapist to avoid any suggestion of premeditated crime, or of her actions being condoned), but also to make sure it contributed to a wider political discourse about the fear of talking about rape, something he believed *Outrage* did not do:

> Our story is just the opposite. It is the effect of a concealment from the world and more important from law enforcement agencies [...] [It] serves as an example to such offenders of how they can continue to get away with such offenses. This is the second service I believe our picture can perform, namely, to educate the public not to conceal such cases, but rather to face the fact and the public gaze, if necessary, with a view toward the greater social good—the eventual lowering of the rate of such offenses.[15]

Dozier's letter makes clear his awareness of the barriers that *The Scar* faced to getting produced, including overcoming the Production Code, the PCA's anxieties about its own reputation, and the prevailing cultural attitudes towards rape. As such, he framed the film as educational and of moral and social importance. But tellingly, Dozier's letter also reveals what the real structural barrier was to *The Scar* being made in its original form: a strong female character. As he concluded in his letter to Breen, 'I think Columbia will not only have a commercial film, but one of which we, and you, may be proud [...] surely we are not going to condemn our girl just because she can speak'.[16]

Dozier's final point—the empowered female voice—needs to be considered alongside the material evidence in the *Case History* file. *The Scar,* and its subsequent revised iterations, is a story about women. And yet, the project's fate, along with how women are represented, was being decided exclusively by men. Just as with *All Flags Flying*, the presence of women, their representation, and the discussion of women's rights were perceived as a threat to moral decency. Following a resubmission of *The Scar* in a revised form—this time the woman kills the rapist out of self-defence rather than as premeditated murder—Breen and Dozier met face-to-face to discuss the challenges faced in producing the project. A memo captures what was discussed between the two at this story conference, including the realisation that *The Scar* would never receive PCA approval:

> Mr Breen spent considerable time in an effort to persuade Mr Dozier to dismiss this story from any further consideration, on the theory that, no matter what refinements or changes may be made in the revised outline, the story is still one of shocking rape, and the results thereof, insofar as these have to do with the girl who was raped.[17]

The memo makes it clear that Breen was still not dismissing *The Scar* on the provisions of the Production Code, but largely based on his experience of *Outrage* and also his own 'personal thought'.[18] This included the opinion that *Outrage* was 'highly distasteful', but that the PCA had felt it needed to be approved 'at that time'.[19] Breen and Dozier were clearly involved in a lengthy discussion about *The Scar*, with Breen pushing the point that the project was not 'entertainment', though, in making this point, Breen seems to have overlooked Dozier's earlier correspondence in which he claimed the film would be educational.

Still, Breen seems to have thought he had convinced Dozier not to pursue *The Scar* any further. But the next document in the file, a memo from April 1951, shows that Columbia had continued to develop the project and submitted a revised treatment by Dozier to the PCA. Once again, Breen urged Columbia to drop the project, convening a meeting with Harry Cohn. And once again, Breen was not citing the Production Code, but rather appealing to the moral sensitivities of Cohn in asking him not to produce the film, saying, 'any story dealing extensively with the mental shock reaction on the part of a girl who had been raped would suggest a very unpleasant theme and an atmosphere which seemed to us to be not good for mixed audiences'.[20] Cohn seems to have been persuaded by Breen's warnings about potential censorship issues overseas, including the likelihood of being 'placed in Category X' in the UK.[21] As such, Cohn agreed to 'forget all about the story'.[22]

The *Case History* file shows that another producer, Jerry Wald—again affiliated to Columbia—revived the project, reworking it in late 1952. In response, the PCA provided Wald with access to the case files for the project, but this did not stop him from looking to produce what had now been renamed *Case History*. A memo of a meeting between

Wald and the PCA's Geoffrey Shurlock indicates how the producer was attempting to frame the story as being one of religious faith and transformation:

> Mr. Wald indicated that he wished to make this the story of a girl who loses her faith as a result of having been raped, and later recovers it. The emphasis will be on the question of faith, and the rape will be merely a springboard, very much as in the case of *Johnny Belinda*.[23]

In taking a more spiritual approach, at least as pitched in the above meeting, Wald convinced the PCA it might be possible for such a picture to be successfully produced and for it to avoid encountering resistance from both foreign censors and wider society.

However, the next document in the file indicates that Wald had perhaps been somewhat misleading in his story pitch. He submitted a 38-page treatment to the PCA in March 1953 for *Case History*, written by Ranald MacDougall. The first five pages detail the rape of the woman, Hazel, in what reads like a Hitchcockian thriller. The scene starts in a shopping mall car park. A petty thief breaks into Hazel's car looking for anything of value he can find. But his crime is disrupted by the return of Hazel and so he hides in the back of the car as she sets off. After a while, he notices that Hazel is driving down a deserted road: 'The road is nearly empty. The young man grins. That suits him. He stares at the back of the girl's head. Pretty'.[24]

Rather than a story of religious transformation, the story becomes a crime thriller, with the rapist even getting hold of Hazel's personal details so he can stalk her. Indeed, there is a real menace about the story, in the style of *Cape Fear* (1962) or *Night of the Hunter* (1955). It verges on horror. The rapist becomes more of a central character, something that is stressed in the preface to the treatment: 'Where do you begin a story like this? Start with him. The God of the Machine. The reason. Not the real beginning of the story. Merely a starting point. The story has no real beginning. And no end'.[25] The approach taken in the revised treatment was in clear contradiction to what Wald suggested to the PCA in his previous meeting. The final document in the file is a memo from April 1953 documenting another meeting between Shurlock and Wald, in which the following was noted:

> The story, as recited to us, was the tale of the girl finding her faith again and being brought back to her former position as a member of society. The treatment we received differed greatly from that

> outlined to us. It was not difficult to point out to these men that there was a vast difference between the story of a girl who regains her faith in humanity, which she lost temporarily because of her unfortunate experience, as opposed to a story which is all about a girl who is raped.[26]

The memo reveals how the discussions once again returned to the precedent set by *Outrage* and the reputational damage suffered by the PCA in the trade press. Shurlock conveyed to the producers how the project, even when not physically portraying rape, was still about the psychological and emotional damage caused by rape and that it 'Would be extremely unwise to present a full-length motion picture based on such subject material'.[27] The memo describes how the producers proceeded to outline solutions to 'eliminate this problem'—the overall connections throughout the film to the act of rape—indicating the insistence of the producers in developing *Case History* as well as the lack of an explicit rejection of the project by the PCA. One creative resolution was to utilise flashbacks in which the girl, following the rape, would keep thinking back to happier times prior to the rape taking place. This would, it was hoped, 'eliminate the harking back time and time again to the act of rape itself'.[28] The memo indicates that all those present at the meeting agreed this to be a potential solution. The final paragraph in the memo states the following:

> The conference concluded with the agreement that we could disregard, for the time begin, that treatment which had been submitted to us, and await a completely revised story outline which should be forthcoming within a few weeks.[29]

With no more evidence available in the *Case History* file, it is not clear whether a revised treatment was submitted to the PCA, whether the documentation is simply missing, or whether the producers ultimately decided that the creative compromises were too much. But what the archival documents do show is, first, the process of creative negotiation that would take place between the PCA and producers. In the initial correspondence, the potential barriers to the film's production were outlined by the PCA, if somewhat vaguely, presenting the producers the opportunity to revise and respond accordingly. Second, the process of creative negotiation left a space for the persistent perusal of the project by different producers over a period of three years. The available documents show that there was a clear interest in representing the topic of rape on screen by producers at Columbia. Third, the documents show how previous produced films could set a precedent for the PCA's subsequent opinions and approval processes, with the organisation repeatedly returning to the indignation caused by a similar film. This precedent even transcended the transition in PCA directors, with the replacement of Breen by Shurlock. What mattered to both was what was in the PCA records, consulting them to inform their decision-making process. What the archival evidence reflects are the organisational processes of the PCA and its unity of thought across administrators and time periods. The organisation kept meticulous records of its interactions with producers and filmmakers, allowing it to understand its own historical reaction to a project as well as how a project had evolved over time. And, fourth, the documents show how producers would, in face-to-face meetings, attempt to convince the PCA of a particular worthwhile creative trajectory for a project, while in reality taking a very different approach. The evidence shows how stories evolved and mutated, often not as the PCA wished, but often in response to individual producer desire, commercial imperative, and the conflicting tension between what the PCA believed audiences wanted and what studios and/or producers believed audiences wanted. Regardless of whether the individual producer's approach to a story was meritorious or not—the *Case History* files indicate both noble ambitions (Dozier) and exploitative motivations (Wald)—the PCA's attitude towards projects that dealt with rape is indicative of wider systemic cultural conditions in the Production Code era and the way women's bodies and women's issues were being controlled by men.

The theme of rape is also the subject of the *Ships in the River* file. The file contains only seven documents (four letters, one memo, and two treatments), but the PCA's unity of thought is once again on display. The file commences with correspondence between Charles Hoffman, of Warner Bros., and Joseph Breen in August 1946. Hoffman submitted a treatment for a project he was hoping to produce with director Michael Curtiz. Hoffman's letter to Breen suggests that the project had a pre-existing relationship beyond the evidence available in the file, with Hoffman remarking that an administrator at the PCA office had previously indicated the 'problem involved in the story'.[30] The pre-existing life of *Ships in the River* is also hinted at by the fact that the treatment submitted to the PCA office is subtitled 'Third Revised Treatment'. Written by Harold Medford, with input from Hoffman and Curtiz, the twenty-page treatment reveals a story that is startlingly similar to *The Scar*/*Case History*. Set in Manhattan, it centres on Karen, a nightclub singer. After being raped, she is reluctant to talk of her experience or to give details to the police of her attacker.

Karen's silence leads to her developing an emotional trauma and a deep-seated fear of men. She falls in love with Johnny, who proposes to her, but Karen dare not accept out of the fear that she has developed of men. As her relationship progresses, she has repeated flashbacks to the night of her violent assault, with the story having at its centre a detailed reconstruction of the rape. The rape sequence is shown from the first-person perspective of the attacker so as to conceal his identity from the audience, and in a bid to incorporate an element of suspense to the story. Presumably, this sequence was written in collaboration with Curtiz, given the way it features directions on how it would be shot, while the problematic nature of what is being portrayed is acknowledged by the author:

> Note: Great care is to be taken that the man himself is not seen, and his emotions are to be indicated but not expressed visually. The situation will be handled with all possible caution and taste.[31]

Karen becomes pregnant after the rape and gives birth to the child, but still refuses to divulge the identity of her attacker, who she apparently knows. She gives up the child for adoption, after which her life falls apart and she becomes estranged from Johnny. The two meet again by chance some years later, with the treatment fixating on the extent of Karen's emotional trauma. She refuses to disclose to Johnny why she disappeared, coming close to an 'emotional collapse' because of her 'frantic determination to tell him nothing'.[32] Johnny calls her crazy, a word that suddenly comes to dominate the narrative:

> The world 'crazy' is like the striking of an alarm, and it rings in Karen's mind as she recoils. With horror in her eyes, she turns, streaks toward the door—and we:
>
> DISSOLVE TO:
>
> An unlighted gas jet, sizzling softly with escaping gas, in Karen's room as—the word 'crazy' mounting in her mind.[33]

Following her emotional breakdown, Karen relocates to a small community in Vermont with the assistance of her doctor, who reunites her with her now grown-up child. She informs Johnny of her decision to move town, who himself decides to relocate as well to the same town, along with his friend Brady, unbeknown to Karen. The story concludes with Johnny and Karen becoming reacquainted, but when he introduces her to his friend Brady, it is revealed that he is the rapist.

Brady tries to attack Karen and her child, but they flee into the woods. A storm rages and as Brady pursues the pair, a tree is struck by lightning, topples over, and kills him. The final scene is of Johnny and Karen marrying, Karen now free of her emotional trauma: 'in contrast to the earlier sequences, everything is sunny, gay, and happy'.[34]

I detail the plot of *Ships in the River* in a bid to draw attention to its similarity to *The Scar/Case History*, from its exploration of the psychological trauma of the rape to the fact it features a Swedish doctor. Could it be that this project was also an adaptation of the Swedish film *The Case of Ingegerd Bremssen*? Quite possible. But the similarities also demonstrate how, in many ways, the *Case History* file is a continuation of the creative discourse that commenced with *Ships in the River*. The PCA was explicit in stating that it could not approve *Ships in the River* in its current form, with the story being 'unacceptable' against the provisions of the Production Code.[35] In a letter to Jack Warner, Breen outlined the PCA's reasoning, stating that *Ships in the River* deals 'rather intimately with the character development of a woman who has been raped and who has given birth to a child. We feel that any such treatment on the subject of rape could not be approved'.[36]

Breen's letter to Warner is polite and he invites him, along with the producers, to discuss the project further at the PCA office. In extending this invite, Breen was hinting towards compromise and the possibility that the project could be approved, but that the problematic elements of it (which Hoffman had already acknowledged) needed to be discussed. What the archival documents reveal is the process of creative negotiation between the producers and the PCA. But the process this time, in contrast to *The Scar*, was fairly straightforward, with a resolution found that satisfied both parties. Yet, the resolution is disturbing. The revised treatment that Breen, the producers, and the screenwriter agreed on made Karen the wife of Brady 'a brutal, drunken husband who mistreats her, and that a legitimate child is born of this unhappy union, rather than born as a result of raping'.[37] This new approach is potentially even more problematic than the original story. The memo that records the conference in which this new story was devised conveys the sense that the men in the meeting agreed that it was perfectly acceptable to legitimise the brutalisation of the female body as long as it occurred within the sanctity of marriage—the 'pure love' as it is referred to in the Production Code. As for Karen's fear of men, or her 'physical revulsion' as the memo terms it, this would 'stem from her unhappy marriage and not from any abhorrence to physical contact with men'.[38] In short, the producers and the PCA were agreeing to control the female body and women's response to men on screen within the framework of their own patriarchal rules.

The control of the female body is not uncommon across the 38 PCA records, even in projects that have very few women in them. Indeed, a standard paragraph sent to producers by the PCA was meant to regulate the presentation of the female body on screen, as in this example from a letter to the independent producer Ben Pivar:

> We wish to direct your particular attention to the need for the greatest possible care in the selection and photographing of the costumes and dresses for your women. The Production Code makes it mandatory that the intimate parts of the body—specifically the breasts of women—be fully covered at all times. Any compromise with this regulation will compel us to withhold approval of your picture.[39]

A theme that emerges from analysing these archival documents is how the structural barrier that contributed to the projects remaining unmade was, in the broadest possible sense, men. At least, that is to say that the structural barrier was not the representation of rape necessarily, but rather men's belief in how women and women's sexuality should and should not be represented on screen, men's framing of the non-lawful abuse of women's bodies (i.e. outside of wedlock), and men's attitudes towards the emotional turmoil women suffer as a result of sexual abuse and assault. As for the violence, cruelty, and domestic abuse suffered in a marriage, that apparently was fine and the PCA would not stand in the way of such a project. If non-consensual sex occurred within the framework of marriage, that was fine too. The organisation did object, however, to the representation of women who visibly reacted to and against mistreatment and domestic abuse suffered in marriage. In *Ships in the River*, once the treatment was revised, the PCA was happy to approve it on the condition that 'the writers keep in mind the necessity of avoiding any pointed references to rape or the effects of rape on the girl', and of avoiding the representation of Karen becoming an alcoholic as a result of the misery of her marriage.[40] Otherwise, the PCA was 'happy' with the basic story, as were the producers.[41]

Like the *Case History* files, the *Ships in the River* files end abruptly. The above letter of approval from Breen to Warner is the last document in the file, with the final paragraph asking the producers to keep the PCA informed as to the development of the project. There is no further evidence as to why the project remained unmade, or at least why it has been categorised as 'unproduced' by the Margaret Herrick Library. In this instance, from the evidence available, it was not because of the story submitted to the PCA, which ultimately was approved.

*

The PCA records analysed in this chapter demonstrate the gaps in evidence when it comes to archival research and the study of the unmade. Either the evidence is incomplete (a lack of creative material, for example) or the records end abruptly, with no further documentation existing as to why projects remained unmade. The records also hint at wider structural forces at work, beyond the PCA, that contributed to projects remaining unmade: internal processes within Hollywood studios, wider attitudes within society, and the misogynistic values of men in power. Arguably, it was the representation of women and of the perceived threat to men by women which contributed to these projects encountering difficulties and remaining unmade. Men were in positions of privilege and power in the PCA and Hollywood studios to determine what or who was represented on screen, how it (rape) or they (women) were represented, or even if they (stories by and about women) were allowed to progress to the point of being considered acceptable for representation on screen. The unmade was, in part, determined by the cultural conditions of the era and of the male desire to control women's bodies and women's issues as they appeared in films.

The patriarchal forces at work are also hinted at by the tone of disrespect in the archival documents. In the case of *All Flags Flying*, the sexism is overt and explicit in the way men talk of and respond to Edna Riley. Men even demean Riley as being unable to comprehend how women behave, how they should be perceived on screen, and how audiences respond to them. Riley was herself a threat, for she spoke out. The issue of female empowerment, and the male want to suppress the voice of women (literally and metaphorically), is something that producer Jerry Wald implicitly suggested in his remark to Joseph Breen: 'surely we are not going to condemn our girl just because she can speak'.[42] In contrast, men are given the utmost respect and are invited to have in-depth discussions about how to conceive of creative solutions to problematic issues concerning women, in particular rape and domestic abuse. What this slim sample of records shows is how it was men that acted as a structural barrier to creativity involving women and contributed to projects like *All Flags Flying* remaining unmade.

Notes

1 Letter from Edna Riley to Cardinal Hayes, September 12, 1934, *All Flags Flying*, PCA records, The Margaret Herrick Library Digital Collection (MHLDC).
2 Letter from Joseph Breen to Will Hays, October 10, 1934, *All Flags Flying*, PCA records, MHLDC.
3 Ibid.
4 Ibid.
5 Report by Karl Lischka, November 8, 1934, *All Flags Flying*, PCA records, MHLDC.
6 Ibid.
7 Letter from Joseph Breen to John Hammell, November 6, 1934, PCA records, MHLDC.
8 *The Scar* outline, September 1950, *Case History*, PCA records, MHLDC.
9 Ibid.
10 Ibid.
11 Letter from Joseph Breen to B. B. Kahane, September 12, 1950, *Case History*, PCA records, MHLDC.
12 Ibid.
13 Ibid.
14 Letter from William Dozier to Joseph Breen, September 19, 1950, PCA records, MHLDC.
15 Ibid.
16 Ibid.
17 Memo for the Files, 'The Scar', September 21, 1950, *Case History*, PCA records, MHLDC.
18 Ibid.
19 Ibid.
20 Memo for the Files, Re. 'The Scar', April 27, 1951, *Case History*, PCA records, MHLDC.
21 Ibid.
22 Ibid.
23 Memo for the Files, Re 'The Case of Ingegerd Bremssen (The Scar) (Columbia)', December 9, 1952, *Case History*, PCA records, MHLDC.
24 *Case History* treatment, March 24, 1953, 5, *Case History*, PCA records, MHLDC.
25 Ibid., preface.
26 Memo for the Files, Re: 'The Scar' (Columbia), April 9, 1953, *Case History*, PCA records, MHLDC.
27 Ibid.
28 Ibid.
29 Ibid.
30 Letter from Charles Hoffman to Joseph Breen, August 8, 1946, *Ships in the River*, PCA records, MHLDC.
31 *Ships in the River* treatment, August 8, 1946, 6, *Ships in the River*, PCA records, MHLDC.
32 Ibid., 6.
33 Ibid., 9.
34 Ibid., 20.

35 Letter from Joseph Breen to Jack Warner, August 13, 1946, *Ships in the River*, PCA records, MHLDC.
36 Ibid.
37 Memo for the Files, Re: Warner Bros 'Ships in the River', August 16, 1946, *Ships in the River*, PCA records, MHLDC.
38 Ibid.
39 Letter from Joseph Breen to Ben Pivar, December 3, 1947, *Santa Fe Uprising*, PCA records, MHLDC.
40 Letter from Joseph Breen to Jack Warner, August 22, 1946, *Ships in the River*, PCA records, MHLDC.
41 Ibid.
42 Dozier to Breen, September 19, 1950.

5 Sex

Themes and representations of sex are present in at least 22 of the 38 Production Code Administration (PCA) records, ranging from adultery and sex 'suggestiveness' (*House of Mist*, *Coquette*, *Love by Force*), prostitution (*Love Child*), abortion and illegitimate child birth (*The Weather in the Streets*), teenage pregnancy (*High School Wives*), to venereal disease (*The Vicious Circle*), nymphomania (*There's One in Every Town*), illicit sex (*Burning Secret*, *Lysistrata*), miscegenation (*Congaï*), and even bestiality (*White Gorilla*). However, while the PCA was always cautious in dealing with themes of sex, going so far as to entirely reject proposals before an outline or script had even been written, it was quite often not the only barrier that led to these films being left unmade. This chapter explores the material evidence of sex in the 38 records in a bid to consider what the unmade PCA records can tell us about the cultural and production conditions of the era.

*

Between the introduction of the Production Code in 1930 and the formation of the PCA in 1934, administrators such as Colonel Jason Joy appear to have been surveying the cultural industries for material that could pose potential future threats to the moral standards of films. For example, archival documents in the *Lysistrata* file show that Joy took the pre-emptive action of ascertaining the suitability of the stage play *Lysistrata* for film adaptation; it was playing at a theatre in Philadelphia in May 1930 and transferring to Broadway in June that year. Archival documents show that an unnamed administrator attended a performance of the play in Philadelphia and wrote a memo to Joy in response. The administrator described the play as an adaptation of an 'ancient Greek classic written by Aristophanes'.[1] The memo succinctly details the story as being about 'militant suffragettes' in Athens,

DOI: 10.4324/9781003206118-5

a group of women determined to bring an end to the war with Sparta.[2] To achieve this, 'all women refuse to *co-habit* with their husbands as long as there is a war'.[3] The results of this weaponised abstinence are ultimately successful, with the war ending and the women able to return to their husbands. The implications of the story are clear: the threat posed by women by the weaponisation of sex. The memo writer suggested that the problem with the play was not the fact that women had become politicised, but rather that they were withholding sex from their husbands. The memo writer suggested that this element of the plot could be substituted: 'It might be possible in a picture to have the wives revolt and refuse to cook, keep house, weave, or do anything for their husbands as well as leaving their beds, thus preventing the pointing of the sex relationship'.[4]

Another Production Code administrator attended a performance of *Lysistrata* in New York in June 1930 and again sent Joy a memo, in which it was confirmed that 'this play cannot be made into a motion picture'.[5] Again, the unnamed administrator emphasised that it was the depiction of the withholding of sex that was the problem, noting,

> I doubt seriously however that the less sophisticated audience outside New York would accept it. [...] It could be done by changing the women's revolt to a domestic revolt of which the idea of having no sex relations is only a part.[6]

The pre-emptive move taken by the Production Code administrators was not about preventing *Lysistrata* from being adapted, but rather about identifying in advance problematic thematic elements related to sex in potential literary material and how these problems could be overcome in any future film adaptation. What caused consternation in relation to *Lysistrata* was how it might disturb audiences through its implication and depiction of men wanting sex and women refusing to have it. There was one particular scene, in which a husband attempts to initiate sex with his wife but she refuses, that was deemed as necessary for elimination in any adaptation. What is perhaps most interesting about these archival documents from 1930 is how the Production Code administrators were clearly attuned to industrial trends and producer ambitions, sensing that production companies would ultimately attempt to adapt plays like *Lysistrata* for the screen.

The *Lysistrata* file indicates that the first attempt to produce a screen adaptation came in late 1934, with RKO Studios expressing an interest. In response, administrators associated with the Production Code avoided stating that an adaptation was prohibited, instead suggesting that it would 'encounter very serious censorship objections [...] in its fundamental motivation'.[7] The fundamental motivation, of course, was sex, or the withholding of sex by women. The producers at RKO (it is not entirely clear from the documentation who it was exactly at RKO that was interested in an adaptation) were informed that they could proceed with an adaptation if they wished, but at their own commercial risk: 'If a company wishes to jeopardize its investment by having its product mutilated by these censors, it is wholly within their own decision'.[8] The Production Code administrators made it clear that, while they accepted some 'adventurous company' might one day successfully adapt the play for the screen, it was 'a very remote possibility'.[9] In other words, the administrators had in their own minds already confined *Lysistrata* to the category of the unmade.

The *Lysistrata* file shows that there were further attempts to adapt the play. In March 1934, shortly after the formation of the PCA, Harry Ginsberg of Hal Roach Studios expressed an interest in the project to Joseph Breen. In an internal note dated March 19, Breen wrote how he had initially advised Ginsberg away from an adaptation of the play, with no indication as to why or on what basis.[10] But Ginsberg's overtures to the PCA indicated a wider interest across the industry in the play. According to a telegram sent to Breen, MGM had registered the title of the play in 1930 and re-registered it in January 1934.[11] Maybe Joy had been aware of this, hence his pre-emptive moves to ascertain its suitability for adaptation. But after the initial contact between Breen and Ginsberg, Breen set out to uncover if there were any specific 'handicaps' that an adaptation of *Lysistrata* would face.[12] Breen sent further correspondence to Henry Ginsberg on March 20, somewhat changing his opinion about the play and the possibilities of an adaptation. Having researched the matter, Breen realised that a number of studios had the play under consideration for adaptation, though none had to date pursued a production. Breen then references Joy's earlier investigations into the play, stating that:

> It is my impression that the general opinion, among those who have made some study of the play, is that it would be acceptable, with some changes, to a highly sophisticated and intelligent audience, but that a less sophisticated audience would be likely to resent it.[13]

Breen was echoing how administrators four years previously had framed *Lysistrata*. The *Lysistrata* file does not contain any evidence of the outcomes of Ginsberg's interest in the play. The final piece of evidence is a one-line memo that simply reads, 'Talked with Hal Roach about LYSISTRATA'.[14]

What the file does show is how, in 1940, producer Boris Morros wrote a treatment of a modernised American version of the play, informing the PCA in January that year of his efforts. Morros confirmed to Breen that *Lysistrata* was 'on my new schedule', had been written by Donald Ogden Stewart, and was to be directed by Rouben Mamoulian.[15] Breen acknowledged this information but requested that a script for the film be submitted before production begins.[16] But once again, the archival trail ends abruptly, with no indication of the outcome of Morros' adaptation.

What these particular files indicate is that, while the PCA clearly had a concern for sex, it wasn't always necessarily the reason for why a film was left unmade. Or at least, not directly. Some producers were happy to be merely warned away from a particular project, while others wanted to push the limits of moral decency on screen, though administrators of the Production Code and later the PCA warned of the potential commercial risks this posed. What seems to have been taking place is a process of horizon scanning, a pre-emptive strategy by the PCA to locate and analyse literary material that could be adapted to ascertain the challenges it posed to the Production Code, to censors, or to the reputation of the industry as a whole. Indeed, *Lysistrata* is not the only example of this process in the 38 records, with other projects being part of the same strategy, including the stage plays *Congai* and *Coquette*. The latter was even in part responsible for the introduction of the Production Code, as Joseph Breen noted in a letter to the producer Merian C. Cooper, who was interested in pursuing an adaptation of the play. The play had previously been adapted for the screen by Mary Pickford in 1928:

> It may be of interest to you to know that, in the discussions, early in 1930, leading up to the adoption of the code, the Pickford picture was cited as a case in point typifying the kind of picture which should *not* be made.[17]

The archival evidence indicates that, in response to Cooper's interest in adapting *Coquette*, Breen initiated a pre-emptive strategy of scanning trade journals to gauge whether, and which, producers were considering pursuing the project. This is clear from a letter Breen sent to S. J. Briskin, a producer at RKO Studios, in January 1937, stating that he had read in the trade papers that 'you are contemplating the purchase of the screen rights to the play, COQUETTE'.[18] Breen described the play as 'highly dangerous', forwarding to Briskin all of the previous correspondence between the PCA and Merian Cooper to make it clear that any adaptation would 'have to be rejected'.[19]

The problem with *Coquette*, and other proposed film projects like it (*House of Mist*, *Love by Force*, *Lysistrata*), was in the 'suggestiveness' of sex, a phrase deployed by the PCA in a letter contained in the *House of Mist* and *Love by Force* files. Indeed, when it comes to the presentation of sex on screen, evidence in the 38 PCA records indicates that it was often the power of coercive persuasion by the PCA that led to projects being radically altered or left unmade, though by no means the only force in this process. Both *House of Mist* and *Love by Force* are similar in this regard. Both projects have similar stories, with narratives of adultery and illicit sex, leading to a protracted process of creative negotiation between the PCA and the producers in order to bring the projects in line with the Production Code. The *House of Mist* file in particular highlights the frustrations this caused for producers. But it must be noted that there is no evidence in the *House of Mist* or *Love by Force* files that this process was *the* reason the projects were left unmade. It is unclear from the material evidence available in the PCA records why these projects were never made.

House of Mist was a project being produced throughout 1946 and 1947 by Hal Wallis Productions, an independent production company affiliated to Paramount Studios. It was to be an adaptation of an unpublished novel (at the time of submission to the PCA) by 'a famous South American author': *The House of Mist* by María Luisa Bombal (1947).[20] The book had already been adapted into a script, written by Ayn Rand, by December 1947, and it was this script that had been submitted to the PCA. There is no document that records a response from the PCA. Instead, the next available document is a letter from Joseph Breen to Hal Wallis recalling the details of a face-to-face meeting between the pair. The letter does not indicate that the script had been rejected, but instead that a conversation had taken place about the representation of the 'adulterous affair between Helga and Landa', which was at the centre of the story.[21] Breen's description of the meeting highlights the process of persuasion used by the PCA to enact creative changes:

> It is our understanding that it is not your intention to indicate that there has been any adulterous affair [...] but that rather, it is your intention to indicate that Helga dreams that she has been unfaithful, and that it is the purpose of her husband to prove to her that she could not have been unfaithful.[22]

Breen listed changes required throughout the script, each time coming back to the point that the story needed to make clear to the audience that 'there has been no illicit sex affair'.[23] Wallis' team revised the script in light of the discussions with the PCA and submitted a revised version in October 1947. In the resubmission letter, the production company emphasised the considerable creative and financial resource being invested into the project in terms of the time taken to rewrite the script.[24] Despite this, the PCA was forthright in its rejection of the script, saying, 'this basic material could not be approved under the provisions of the Production Code because of the fact that it treats the theme of adultery in a too intimate and detailed a manner'.[25] The problem stemmed from the fact that the new script persistently dwelled on the act of adultery, with the main characters discussing throughout the story whether Helga had an affair or not, or whether she had just dreamed it. Breen concluded, 'This is pursued in an extremely detailed manner which we feel will certainly cause offense'.[26]

Adultery is a common theme across many of the 38 PCA records containing stories of or featuring sex, and it was persistently something that the PCA wanted to eliminate references to via the process of creative negotiation. Yet, this process could lead to both contradiction and misinterpretation, as seems to be the case in *House of Mist*. Breen's letter to Wallis in January 1947, in response to the first draft script, seems to suggest that it had been the PCA that had recommended a revised story focusing on discussions of whether or not an affair took place. But by October 1947, this was viewed by the PCA to be the main problem of the story, despite the archival evidence indicating the PCA had suggested this solution. The process of creative negotiation also seemed to leave open spaces for interpretation of what the PCA was actually saying. After all, Breen's January 1947 letter to Wallis is in fact quite vague, only noting that 'it is not your intention to indicate that there has been an adulterous affair', rather than stating outright that the discussions of adultery were unacceptable.[27]

The process of creative negotiation could ultimately lead to a story being radically changed from the one originally envisaged by the producer. As such, even if there is no direct evidence of why a project was not made, it could be argued that a project, in its original, 'raw' state as submitted to the PCA, was often left unmade as a result of this process. That is certainly the case with *House of Mist*. The first script submitted to the PCA, an adaptation of a novel, was gradually being transformed through a protracted series of meetings, to the point that Hal Wallis believed a wholly different story had emerged some nineteen months later (with at least two more revised scripts being written) in July 1948, at which point the script was approved for production. The problem with *House of Mist* was that the characters were debating whether an affair took place or not, which by implication meant that the characters were actually talking about whether the main character 'engaged in sexual intercourse'.[28] Even if the story concluded by emphasising that no affair had taken place and was nothing more than a dream, the problem remained that the main character was fantasising about engaging in sexual intercourse. For Hal Wallis, however, the PCA was causing unnecessary frustration and confusion of its own interpretation of sex as judged against the provisions of the Production Code:

> We have made every change suggested by them to bring this script within *their* [PCA's] interpretation of the Code, despite our disagreement with the points raised and the script of October 16 [...] meets *their* [PCA's] final objections which I must take to be the opinion of your office. The Code Administration is a continuing body. Inasmuch as we have violently wrenched our script to satisfy the Code Administration, I cannot accept your contention that the rulings of your associates have no validity and that I must discard a full year's work.[29]

Wallis' letter is evidence of how the process of creative negotiation impacted the financial resources of producers and production companies, particularly when a script was being regularly rejected, despite a producer claiming to have implemented all recommended revisions. Wallis' frustrations seemed to stem from miscommunication, with the PCA wanting the total elimination of reference to a *sexual* affair:

> The important factual point in the script upon which we were all in agreement is the fact, as we see it, that your female lead, Helga, engages in an illicit sex affair. [...] This being so, the solution of the major problem, from our standpoint should be very simple, namely to clear up any doubt that Helga engaged in an illicit sex affair and affirmatively establish that her only transgression was the violation of the Code that existed among her people, which highly condemned a married woman who would go alone to the home of a man not her husband.[30]

Of course, by removing the element of sex from the affair, a very different story was being told. It became, as the PCA indicated, a story about the violation of the 'code of social conduct of the mores of the place and times of the story'.[31] In effect, *House of Mist* would become a story about the dangers of straying from the principles of moral decency set out in the Production Code. As for any engagement in or thoughts of sex by the main character, a new solution was proposed: an onscreen kiss, which would 'symbolize' a breaking of the cultural mores of the society the characters inhabit.[32] Following this change, along with changes to suggestive dialogue, the PCA approved the script on July 7, 1948, at which point the archival documentation ends.[33]

*

What the 38 PCA records leave behind is a trace of a discourse about the media effects, and meaning, of sex. What remains is a discourse related to the cultural conditions of the era and of how sex contributed to intense debate, confusion, and anger on the part of producers, screenwriters, and the PCA. Indeed, the latter was acutely aware of a need to balance the commercial imperatives of producers wanting to sell films via the sex appeal of their most glamorous stars versus the social imperatives of upholding moral decency as set out by the Production Code.

One particular aspect of sex that caused grave consternation for all concerned was prostitution and casual sex, a prominent feature of *There's One in Every Town*. The problems that this project faced were summed up in a memo from June 1951:

> The present material is *basically* unacceptable under the Code, inasmuch as it was a story of a young girl of fifteen who, in order to make herself accepted in a small Southern town, indulges in a career of wild promiscuity that is little short of a kind of nymphomania.[34]

The presence of the word 'basically' seems to indicate that the barrier to production in the case of this project, and others where the word is used, was the PCA. 'Basically' indicates that the project is highly problematic and that even the process of creative negotiation would not necessarily lead to approval from the PCA. *There's One in Every Town* was being produced by David Hempstead for Twentieth Century-Fox and was an adaptation of the novel of the same name by James Aswell published in 1951. The project had not yet been scripted, with the novel itself being the material on which the PCA was basing its initial reaction. However, Hempstead's project faced numerous problems in that it contained 'an orgy of sex affairs, lesbianism, abortion, and murder'.[35] Yet, interestingly, despite all of these obvious problems pertaining to the representation of sex, an internal PCA memo shows that Twentieth Century-Fox had been advised to proceed in developing a treatment, deeming it 'worth whatever gamble might be involved financially to see if a proper treatment could be salvaged from the present book'.[36]

Twentieth Century-Fox had an option on the book until September 1951, perhaps indicating why the producers endeavoured to persevere with writing a treatment. However, the resultant story was still unacceptable, according to a letter sent from Twentieth Century-Fox to the PCA.[37] The original producer, David Hempstead, had given up on the project and it had been taken over by Nunally Johnson who was insisting that the studio renew the option on the book. Johnson was, according to an internal Twentieth Century-Fox memo forwarded to the PCA, determined to produce a film that was 'the account of a small town tart, and if that one fundamental fact is unacceptable, I would not have any further interest in doing it'.[38] Johnson explained that the story would not be unnecessarily gratuitous in its portrayal of sex:

> I should like to show, step by step, this extremely dangerous route that she takes, from allowing herself to be picked up at a soda fountain, to the late dates, the honking of the horn outside of her home, etc. I should like to show these steps growing more and more ominous. At bottom it is a morality tract. It would be an object lesson on what a young girl should not do. It should be plain almost from the beginning of the picture that such a way of life can lead only to tragedy.[39]

But time and again, Johnson returned to the phrase 'small town tart', which itself seemed to become the problem that both Twentieth Century-Fox and the PCA could not overcome, regardless of Johnson's wider moral intentions for the story. As the PCA indicated in a letter to Twentieth Century-Fox, even when removing all the problem elements of sex, if Johnson was intent on producing a story about a 'town tart' then the story would remain 'basically unacceptable'.[40] The PCA's letter in response to Johnson's proposal reintroduces the word 'basically': this project could *not* be produced and would remain unmade.

*

The presence of permissiveness or 'unusual' sex was of paramount concern for the PCA, with a desire to remove any such material from potential productions. *White Gorilla*, for example, was deemed to possess an 'unacceptable flavor' in that it depicted bestiality: the 'mating of a white woman and a gorilla'.[41] Removal of this element of the story would be enough to satisfy the PCA. *The Vicious Circle* was deemed inappropriate for its explicit depiction of venereal disease, which was strictly prohibited under the provisions of the Production Code. *The Weather in the Streets*, an adaptation of the novel of the same name by Rosamund Lehman from 1936, is the story of a woman who is bored with her marriage and so sleeps with another man, resulting in an illegitimate child and abortion. The story was seen as being 'sordid', particularly in its depiction of casual sex, adultery, and abortion. And *Burning Secret* was, in its first submission to the PCA in 1934, considered 'very dangerous' for its portrayal of a hidden world of sex and of its story of how 'a child learns of the "facts of life" by observing the build-up of an affair between his mother and a chance acquaintance'.[42]

Burning Secret is one of several unmade projects in the 38 PCA records that have stories involving an intersection between sex and children. Others include *Love Child*, a story of a wealthy man that pays a young girl to have a child with him out of wedlock, and *High School Wives*, a social problem drama about illegal teenage marriage and teenage pregnancy. Both of these projects were rejected outright by the PCA for the very fact that children and teenagers themselves were implicated or partaking in sexual acts. *Burning Secret*, however, was pursued by several producers between 1934 and 1964, the extant timeframe of material evidence available in the PCA records. The fourteen available documents in the *Burning Secret* file show that five producers/production companies investigated the possibility of adapting *Burning Secret* to the screen during this time period: Harry Zehner at Universal (1934), Walter McEwan at Warner Bros. (1936), Twentieth Century-Fox (1947), Harris-Kubrick Pictures Corporation on behalf of MGM (1956), and Robert Vogel at MGM (1964) (the archival documentation suggests that these last two attempts both involved Robert Vogel).

Burning Secret was a planned adaptation of Stefan Zweig's novel of the same name (German title of *Brennendes Geheimniss*). The PCA initially disapproved of any attempts to adapt the novel between 1934 and 1956. But between 1956 and 1964, it shifted its position from framing the novel as highly dangerous to viewing it as being 'acceptable as subject matter for a film'.[43] So what occurred to allow the PCA to move from being a barrier to the book's adaptation to an enabler of the project's production? The archival evidence indicates that it was most likely a result of a relaxing of attitudes in society as a whole, with the cultural conditions opening a space for a book like *Burning Secret* to be adapted.

The original verdict on *Burning Secret* in 1934 was that it would be 'impossible' to adapt for its depiction of an illicit sex affair between two adults, which is viewed from the perspective of an adolescent boy and awakening him to the realities of sexual desire.[44] There was little beyond this basic judgement of the unsuitability of the book's adaptation, with Breen repeating the original verdict from 1934 across three separate enquiries through to 1947. Each time, the PCA uses the words 'basic' and 'basically' to refer to the plot of a child witnessing an affair and learning of the 'facts of life'.[45] This seems to indicate that the PCA was not prepared to go any further in discussions of the book with producers and was warning them away from attempting to adapt it, which proved an effective strategy.

By 1956, however, the PCA changed its opinion. And the evidence suggests this was a result of actually re-reading the novel, which does not seem to have occurred since its original submission to the organisation in 1934: the previous rejections of the book were based on the original report by the PCA, not on re-reading the novel or considering individual producers' approaches. The evidence for the attempts to produce *Burning Secret* in 1956 and 1964 is limited, with only a memo and a letter available. In June 1956, the PCA had a meeting with Robert Vogel of MGM, who had submitted the book on behalf of the Harris-Kubrick Pictures Corporation. The PCA concluded that 'On reading it we find that it contains no playing around with a child's curiosity about sex'.[46] This new interpretation was based on the fact that the story could be told from the child's viewpoint with all elements of sex removed. The story could instead be focused on 'the child's fear that the seducer is going to murder his mother, or do some bodily harm to her, devoid of any sex curiosity'.[47] In other words, the PCA did not consider the novel to be about the 'facts of life' and expected producers to hold the same opinion. As such, the PCA removed any objections it had to enable *Burning Secret* to be produced, should a producer want to do so. However, the archival documentation for both the 1956 and the 1964 attempts at adapting the book are incomplete, with no evidence of why the project remained unmade.

*

The 38 records show that the PCA could have been a substantial barrier to films being produced that were about or portrayed illicit, passionate, or unlawful sex, sexual acts, or activities related to sex. However, the records also suggest that the PCA was *not* the primary barrier to scripts being produced that had resulted from the process of creative negotiation. Other forces impacted on the decisions of producers, production companies, and studios, likely ranging from commitments to other projects, commercial risks, or even just a lack of enthusiasm for the revised project. The latter could be seen as an indirect result of the PCA's creative negotiation.

Sex was, however, an issue that led to frustration, confusion, and misinterpretation between all those involved. And it must be noted that the archival evidence was, in the cases cited, all generated by men. In other words, it is possible to start considering the material evidence of the unmade more broadly and to argue that, across those files that in some way reference women or sex, it is the prevailing patriarchal cultural attitudes of the era that are the actual structural barrier contributing to the unmade, rather than any one particular organisation. All male producers, screenwriters, PCA administrators, studio heads, and studio administrators were (still are?), among many others, complicit in perpetuating a discourse of sex and women as a danger to society and in ensuring that Hollywood output furthered patriarchal hegemony.

Notes

1 Memo to Jason Joy, May 15, 1930, *Lysistrata*, PCA records, The Margaret Herrick Library Digital Collection (MHLDC).
2 Ibid.
3 Ibid.
4 Ibid.
5 Memo to Jason Joy, June 11, 1930, *Lysistrata*, PCA records, MHLDC.
6 Ibid.
7 Letter to Gilbert Sedes, October 21, 1930, *Lysistrata*, PCA records, MHLDC.
8 Ibid.
9 Ibid.
10 Resume (Breen), March 19, 1934, *Lysistrata*, PCA records, MHLDC.
11 Telegram from Maurice McKenzie to Joseph Breen, March 1934, *Lysistrata*, PCA records, MHLDC.
12 Telegram from Joseph Breen to Maurice McKenzie, March 19, 1934, *Lysistrata*, PCA records, MHLDC.
13 Letter from Joseph Breen to Henry Ginsberg, March 20, 1934, *Lysistrata*, PCA records, MHLDC.
14 Resume, April 23, 1934, *Lysistrata*, PCA records, MHLDC.
15 Letter from Boris Morris to Joseph Breen, January 9, 1940, *Lysistrata*, PCA records, MHLDC.
16 Letter from Joseph Breen to Boris Morros, January 10, 1940, *Lysistrata*, PCA records, MHLDC.
17 Letter from Joseph Breen to Merian C. Cooper, April 14, 1936, *Coquette*, PCA records, MHLDC.
18 Letter from Joseph Breen to S. J. Briskin, January 11, 1937, *Coquette*, PCA records, MHLDC.

19 Ibid.
20 Letter from John Mock to Joseph Breen, December 27, 1946, *House of Mist*, PCA records, MHLDC.
21 Letter from Joseph Breen to Hal Wallis, January 13, 1947, *House of Mist*, PCA records, MHLDC.
22 Ibid.
23 Ibid.
24 Letter from John Mock to Joseph Breen, October 23, 1947, *House of Mist*, PCA records, MHLDC.
25 Letter from Joseph Breen to Hal Wallis, October 29, 1947, *House of Mist*, PCA records, MHLDC.
26 Ibid.
27 Breen to Wallis, January 13, 1947.
28 Letter from Stephen Jackson to Hal Wallis, December 26, 1947, *House of Mist*, PCA records, MHLDC.
29 Letter from Hal Wallis to Stephen Jackson, December 30, 1947, *House of Mist*, PCA records, MHLDC.
30 Letter from Stephen Jackson to Hal Wallis, December 30, 1947, *House of Mist*, PCA records, MHLDC.
31 Ibid.
32 Memo for the Files, Re: 'House of Mist', January 7, 1948, *House of Mist*, PCA records, MHLDC.
33 Letter from Stephen Jackson to Hal Wallis, July 7, 1948, *House of Mist*, PCA records, MHLDC.
34 Memo for the Files: Re 'There's One in Every Town', June 5, 1951, *There's One in Every Town*, PCA records, MHLDC.
35 Ibid.
36 Ibid.
37 Letter from Jason Joy to Joseph Breen, September 12, 1951, *There's One in Every Town*, PCA records, MHLDC.
38 Nunally Johnson to Jason Joy, Internal Twentieth Century-Fox Memo, September 11, 1951, *There's One in Every Town*, PCA records, MHLDC.
39 Ibid.
40 Letter from Joseph Breen to Jason Joy, November 2, 1951, *There's One in Every Town*, PCA records, MHLDC.
41 Letter from Joseph Breen to A. W. Hackel, May 25, 1944, *White Gorilla*, PCA records, MHLDC.
42 Letter from Joseph Breen to Harry Zehner, January 26, 1934, *Burning Secret*, PCA records, MHLDC.
43 Memo for the Files, Re: 'The Burning Secret', June 11, 1956, *Burning Secret*, PCA records, Margaret MHLDC.
44 Memo for the Files, 'Burning Secret', January 24, 1934, *Burning Secret*, PCA records, MHLDC.
45 Letter from Joseph Breen to Jack Warner, September 2, 1936, *Burning Secret*, PCA records, MHLDC; Letter from Stephen Jackson to Jason Joy, December 10, 1947, *Burning Secret* file, PCA records, MHLDC.
46 'The Burning Secret', June 11, 1956.
47 Ibid.

6 Politics

If the last chapter was evidence of patriarchal hegemony as a structural force contributing to the prevalence of unmade films, this chapter is about how those same forces sought to ensure the hegemony of American capitalism and world order. It is about politics, in the broadest possible sense, for across the 38 Production Code Administration (PCA) records there is repeated evidence of vested interests and powerful forces that pressured the PCA and film producers to prevent certain stories being told on film. The PCA even acknowledged there was a desire by some to ensure film projects remained unmade, what Jason Joy deemed the 'un-doable stories'.[1] What made them un-doable is debatable, though the problems faced by projects such as *Congai*, *Circus Parade*, *Child Labour*, *The Forty Days of Musa Dagh*, *Joan of Arc*, and *Spy Ships* relate to powerful political forces within the US government, the US military, influential trade organisations and trade unions, foreign governments, and the Catholic Church. These forces did not all have the same interest at heart in ensuring stories remained 'un-doable', given that trade union stakeholders likely had very different motives to the US military, but they all had one thing in common: a desire to ensure the representation of their own interests on screen in a favourable light, or otherwise to block the production of a project. What remains in the 38 PCA records are the material traces of these vested political interests and their contribution to the unmade.

*

Circus Parade is one of the earliest dated files among the 38 PCA records. The documentation spans 1928 to 1929, a period prior to the introduction of the Production Code or the formation of the PCA. However, it is a case file that is instrumental in demonstrating the way in which powerful political forces enacted pressure on Hollywood to

DOI: 10.4324/9781003206118-6

prevent a film from being produced. The file comprises twenty-seven documents: twenty-six are some form of correspondence and one is an internal note. While there is no creative material, the shape the file takes in terms of correspondence indicates the level of interaction amongst concerned stakeholders. The two forces that interact throughout the *Circus Parade* file are the Motion Picture Producers & Distributors of America (MPPDA)—the eventual parent organisation to the PCA—and the Circus Fans Association of America (CFAA).

The first document in the *Circus Parade* file is a letter from Maurice McKenzie (assistant to Will Hays) to Jason Joy, dated October 1928. McKenzie explains in the letter that the MPPDA has received a complaint from the CFAA and asks Joy to keep it in mind, but that the complaint did not present a particular problem at that moment in time. Attached to McKenzie's letter is the complaint from the CFAA, submitted by the organisation's secretary-treasurer, Karl Kae Knecht. As McKenzie explained, 'Every now and then we hear from him [Knecht] on matters affecting circuses, usually in a fair-minded way'.[2] However, it is clear that Knecht's letter was far from being fair-minded. He was instead urging the prevention of any adaptation of Jim Tully's novel *Circus Parade* (1927):

> I cannot see how it could be filmed. No filthier or dirtier book had ever been printed, and it is that which sold the book, and without it it is nothing but a lot of mis-represented and farfetched events with wrong details of circus life.[3]

Knecht's concerns related to the way circus life was being portrayed in a negative light in the book. As Knecht noted,

> very little, if any, mention is made of the performers or the performances of a circus or of a circus parade. And so I do not see how it could be used in a film, unless just the title were retained.[4]

The letter from Knecht was kept on file for purposes of using it should a production company consider adapting Tully's book, though McKenzie doubted that 'any of our production companies will undertake it, for I think they are able to find circus stories which are very much more acceptable than the one which Tully wrote'.[5]

There is no evidence of further contact between the MPPDA and the CFAA for another twelve months. However, by October 1929 rumours were circulating in the trade press that a production company had decided to adapt Tully's book. As Maurice McKenzie confided in a letter to Jason Joy, having read the rumours in the *Exhibitors' Daily Review* on October 25, 'somehow I find it unable to keep from fearing difficulties here'.[6] The MPPDA confirmed to Joy that it was registering the title of Tully's book on behalf of Sono-Art Productions, noting that this would 'make a good deal of trouble with circus people and others'.[7] The move by Sono-Art Productions led the MPPDA to invite the film's producer, Jimmy Cruze, to submit a script of the proposed production for independent advice on its suitability.[8] Of course, this being prior to the existence of the Production Code or the PCA, Cruze was under no obligation to do so. Joy explained his anxieties about the situation to McKenzie, stating that he was concerned about Cruze's planned adaptation, in particular because he was an independent producer:

> Inasmuch as Cruze is producing independently for Sono-Art for release through World Wide, it occurs to me offhand that the only way we can handle the situation is to have Mr. Hays intercede through Jim Tully. Undoubtedly Mr. Hays could induce Mr. Tully to submit the script to us for censorship criticism before Mr. Cruze began production and in this manner we might be able to rid it of most of the dirt.[9]

What ensued over the course of October and December 1929 were frantic attempts by the MPPDA to convince Cruze to submit his script for censorship consideration, to little avail. However, it was not Hays that interceded in the first instance, as Joy hoped he would, but rather Frank Wilstach. Wilstach had dinner with Jim Tully, the book's author, in late October 1929, to discuss Cruze's planned adaptation. The aim was to convince Tully himself to talk to Cruze and bring him around to cooperating with the MPPDA.[10] Wilstach's conversation with Tully revealed that Cruze planned to make a film similar to one he had previously directed, *Covered Wagon* (1923). Cruze also wanted the film to feature a 'big scene [...] a circus fight'.[11] Wilstach was assured by Tully that Cruze's adaptation would not be 'offensive to anyone'.[12]

Wilstach's overtures to Tully, and the apparent cooperation it could lead to with Cruze, pleased the MPPDA. Joy himself confirmed that 'If Tully can only convince Cruze of the advisability of tying in with us on this production, I feel that our major worries will be taken care of'.[13] However, there was no contact from Cruze and, by mid-November 1929, Joy believed that 'Jim Tully is giving you [Wilstach] the runaround'.[14] Without cooperation, the worries Joy was referring to soon became apparent: the CFAA's lawyer, and chairman of its legislative committee, contacted the MPPDA to demand to know what action was being taken to prevent *Circus Parade* from being produced, or at the very least to stop any adaptation portraying circuses in a negative way.[15] Wilstach and Joy both hoped that the letter from the CFAA's lawyer would act as the catalyst to bring Cruze around to working with them: 'All of this may serve to bring Jim and Cruze to a realization that they are fooling with dynamite; that is, if they don't take counsel on the story'.[16]

The problem, as the CFAA's lawyer framed it, was in the representation of the circus as a hotbed of crime and deprivation:

> The leading incident of this book [*Circus Parade*], which pretends to be a story of the circus, consists of a roustabout who places a colored girl in a circus wagon and then charges admission to some forty or fifty bums to have relations with her. It is just such horrible stories as these which make me wonder just what we are coming to. The age of the criminal has gone from 34 to 19. The Chief Probation Officer of New York condemns heartily moving picture stories which lead to crime by giving a false view of life. Knowing and respecting what you are trying to do, I beg that you make every effort to prevent the filming of this vicious, ignorant, and outrageous book.[17]

The letter from the CFAA lawyer seems to have had a countereffect, with Wilstach himself becoming enraged at the censorious pressure being enacted by one organisation, which he thought was itself being hypocritical. From Wilstach's perspective, the issue was not necessarily that the book was misrepresentative, but rather that it presented a viewpoint of the circus that the CFAA simply did not want to see onscreen out of fear of the reputational damage it could cause. The pressure being applied by the CFAA related to perception management: that films about circuses should always comply, regardless of the reality, with the wholesome vision that the CFAA wanted to project. As such, the CFAA was itself the barrier to production.

Wilstach decided to confront the CFAA about its hypocrisy, responding to the lawyer's letter by explaining that his own experience of circuses was that they were often 'morally dubious', which was the entire point of Tully's book: to reflect the experience of 'old-time-circus life'.[18] He went so far as to cite examples:

> It was not so long ago, for instance, that one of the big circuses from my home state, Indiana, carried around a car fully equipped with gambling appliances. [...] Only last year, I saw a circus at

> Poughkeepsie, New York, at which, in the side-show, there were a half dozen gambling devices in full operation. I am very glad that Jim Tully hasn't any of these things in his book. But you cannot have a real story of the circus without gambling, and without fights between proprietors, as well as fights between circus people, and town rowdies.[19]

Wilstach was attempting to defend the planned adaptation of *Circus Parade*, while also trying to reassure the CFAA. But he was fighting a losing battle as the CFAA had begun to coordinate a mail-in campaign, with its members from across the USA sending letters of protest to the offices of Will Hays and Jim Tully. Over 500 letters were received as part of the chain-letter protest, though many of those writing in acknowledged they had never read Jim Tully's book and had no awareness of what Cruze planned for his adaptation.[20] The tone of the letters frustrated Wilstach:

> The General [Will Hays] is getting letters from presidents of railroads, governors of states, and one person or another from all over the United States, demanding that the filming of this story be suppressed. Of course, these people imagine that Mr. Cruze is going to put in this picture all of Jim's incarnadine incidents. I am answering all these people, but I must say that when they insist that this 'Circus Parade' should be a 'true story of modern circusdom', I am for getting up on my hind legs and bellowing![21]

Wilstach did not hold back in his response to the chain-letter protests, writing to individual members of the CFAA on a personal basis. An example of one such response was forwarded to Jason Joy:

> It seems to be the general disposition of the circus fans to object to anything in the way of a circus picture, excepting one that portrays the high-class circus of modern times. [...] as to the one point which has been made here, suppose for instance, that many of the people in the various walks of life should set up the cry: 'you must not put anything in books, plays, or motion pictures, except that which treats of the subject we are interested in, in the most favourable light'; that is the same as saying, 'we don't want any story of us except in our purified state'.[22]

Wilstach's points in response to the chain-letters were not necessarily disputed by those that sent them. Responding to Wilstach, the secretary of the Connecticut branch of the CFAA agreed that the aim was to ensure that circuses were represented as 'good, clean amusement'.[23] Anything less than such a positive representation of circus lift would lead to a coordinated campaign by the CFAA to block any attempts at producing *Circus Parade*. As the branch secretary commented,

> You can depend on this—if 'Circus Parade' is a clean, true story of modern circusdom the members of C.F.A. will do their parts toward giving it publicity [...] for every bit of good circus literature helps both the circus and the C.F.A.[24]

The CFAA clearly understood the power of film to create perceptions and effects in audiences and as such was aiming to manipulate how its own industry was being portrayed. Obstinately refusing to overcome the fact that the story was in conflict with its vision of what present-day circus life was about, the CFAA was coordinating efforts to ensure Cruze's production remained unmade. A large part of the problem seemed to stem from confusion about the time period in which the film would be set. Wilstach repeatedly emphasised that Cruze's adaptation was a story about old-time circus life, something the CFAA refused to acknowledge, instead focusing its attention on pushing for an adaptation of *Circus Parade* centred on modern circusdom.

The archival evidence ends with a letter from Wilstach to Joy, one which is somewhat despondent in tone. The letter reads as if Wilstach is overwhelmed by how out of control the situation had become, telling Joy that Hays' office has been inundated with letters of complaint about the adaptation from 'many important people'[25]; the names of these people remain anonymous, though Wilstach's language makes it sound quite ominous that such figures were now involved in the problem. The only way out in Wilstach's opinion was if Cruze himself wrote a letter of explanation to Hays in which he emphatically declared that *Circus Parade* would be 'free of any possible offense'.[26] The letter would then have to be reproduced and circulated to all of the chain-letter writers and the 'many important people' who had contacted Hays.[27]

With the archival trail coming to an end at this point—at least in the PCA records—it is unclear as to whether or not Cruze wrote the letter that Wilstach had proposed, or how far his adaptation of *Circus Parade* actually got. But the case study is fascinating for it reveals how powerful private lobbying interests in the USA were prepared to use their unity of strength and coordinated networks to act as a barrier to the production of a film. The reason *Circus Parade* remained unmade, even with the lack of concluding archival evidence, is quite clearly because of an industry association determined to protect the commercial interests of its members. The case study is also fascinating in how it reveals that the 'censors' themselves—in this case, the Hays office—felt that the CFAA was a hypocritical organisation, wanting a reality reflected on screen that did not necessarily fit with the reality of circus life. Such an approach indicated a dangerous precedent and demonstrated how the censorious behaviour of vested political interests could get out of control.

*

If *Circus Parade* demonstrates the impact of a private organisation on unmade films, there are examples in the 38 records of the way public bodies and/or the government could also have a similar impact. This seems to have been particularly the case with those films that alluded to World War Two or Nazi Germany. Projects such as *Cry Havoc* and *School for Barbarians* present alternate histories of World War Two, or of imagined realities and lands that are clear suggestions of the war in Europe. Projects such as *Two against Tomorrow* and *Spy Ships* were stories of military campaigns or espionage during the war. These were the projects that caused most consternation with politicians and the military, both in the USA and overseas, with repeated attempts to ensure they remained unmade. These attempts can be partially situated in the wider campaign against anti-Nazi Hollywood films led by Senator Gerald Nye, culminating in the 1941 Senate Investigation into Motion Picture Propaganda (Yogerst 2020).

Spy Ships is a particular example of the censorious behaviour of the US government and the US Navy. The project originated in January 1938 as *Navy Spy* and was being produced by Wilford Deming Jr. for the General Pictures Corporation. As Deming told the PCA in his original submission letter, the treatment was informed by extensive discussions with 'high Naval officers'.[28] Alongside wanting the approval of the PCA, Deming also wanted the approval of the US Navy. Deming was forced to resubmit the script via an alternative production company after the PCA informed him that General Pictures Corporation did not appear to be an active business anymore and therefore did not fall under the provisions of the Production Code.[29] A month later, in February 1938, the project was resubmitted via Harry Sherman Productions.[30] The story told of the dangers of fishing fleets, organised by immigrants, along the west coast of the USA. Largely taking place around the harbours of San Pedro, the story focuses on the relationship between the fishing fleets and the battleships they must navigate around. The immigrants include Japanese spies that provide reports to naval intelligence of an impending attack against the US Navy at San Pedro. The story clearly came at a sensitive time in global politics, just one year before the outbreak of war in Europe and with mounting tensions in the Pacific. As the original reader's report of the project noted, 'There are some Japanese spies but some dialogue and a forward to the effect that these spies are *not* representative to the Japanese government'.[31]

The story, as pitched to the PCA, was deemed acceptable and the organisation saw no reason as to why it could not be approved. The barrier to the film's production was not the PCA, however, but the US Navy, as Breen informed Harry Sherman: 'As you know, pictures dealing with the United States Navy, or pictures containing stock shots made at any time with Naval cooperation, must be submitted to the Naval Board in Washington D.C., for their approval'.[32] The reaction from the US Navy Motion Picture Board was swift, with a report sent to the PCA on February 15, just one week after the treatment had been forwarded to the Naval Board for approval. It was not good news: 'The Board feels that this story is dynamite at this time; that it is plainly anti-Japanese and pro-British and would offend a foreign government'.[33] While the PCA had not requested the cooperation of the US Navy on the project, the Board made it clear that 'if the picture was made without naval cooperation, it would have severe repercussions in Washington'.[34] The objection of the US Navy was clear. The Board even acknowledged that Deming had collaborated with naval officers in writing the treatment, but it was feared that this could give the impression of a Navy-authorised film, which it was not. The Board's letter concluded that the US Navy was 'quite definite in its objections to it'.[35]

With such an emphatic verdict on the project, there appeared to be no recourse for its production, to the obvious frustration of Deming. He sent a lengthy two-page letter to the Chairman of the US Navy Motion Picture Board on February 24 to plead his case, or, as he said, 'to remove the objection of your Board'.[36] Deming's letter was the first of several between him, the US Navy Motion Picture Board, and the PCA. The letters demonstrate the impossibility of an independent producer and screenwriter like Deming in overcoming structural barriers put in place by large, politically motivated organisations. The US Navy was simply unmoving in its judgement, even when Deming implored that his film was being made out of patriotic duty: 'this story, properly presented to the American Public as a motion picture, can surely be no less than a patriotic service on the part of the producers, for today there is every reason to awaken Americans to their Navy'.[37] Deming's petition to patriotism indicates how he believed that the barrier standing in the way to *Navy Spy* being produced was a need for absolute allegiance to the American flag. But that was not the issue. In fact, the US Navy did not even want to get into the specifics of why the film should remain unmade, with a letter in response to Deming merely stating that if *Navy Spy* were produced it would be met with 'serious objection'.[38] Following this response, Deming realised that the real barrier was the vested political interest of the US Navy. He subsequently informed the US Navy Motion Picture Board of this belief and of his hope that *Navy Spy* could still be given approval:

> The writer finds no grounds for official Navy Department objection to the story, and it is believed that objection must lie on political grounds, toward which a lenient attitude is requested, that the picture may be produced to serve a patriotic purpose.[39]

Deming tried resurrecting the project in July 1938, now retitled *Spy Ships* (perhaps renamed in a bid to remove the connection to the US Navy) and being produced by Fine Arts Studio. But his efforts were to little avail.[40] The blanket objection of the US Navy remained, essentially consigning the project to the category of the unmade forevermore.

*

In contrast to how the objection of a branch of the US Armed Forces to the production of *Navy Ship* was unwelcomed by its producer, *School for Barbarians* involved a producer that was actively encouraging rejection in a bid to ensure his own project would remain unmade. This may well have been a result of timing, with *School for Barbarians* emerging as a project in August 1939, on the eve of the outbreak of war in Europe. It was a project being produced by Edward Small Productions and there was a tone of nervous tension in the original submission letter sent to Joseph Breen: 'I am anxious to get your reaction as quickly as possible. I would appreciate it very much if you could assign someone to this immediately so that we may get an early report on the story'.[41]

The archival evidence for *School for Barbarians* indicates a strange series of motivations at work on the project, with Edward Small seemingly wanting a rejection of *School for Barbarians*. It is possible to get a sense of the story of *School for Barbarians* via a reader's report of the submitted script. The reader's report conveys the impression that *School for Barbarians* was an unusual story:

> This story concerns the debasement of the children of a normal German village, when the Nazis enter and take over the religious and educational activities. It indicates that when this happens, the normal family life is wrecked and the children are set against their parents. The boys, ten to fourteen years old, are shown being enlisted in the Hitler Youth, given guns and uniforms, and made to drill at all hours of the day and night.[42]

School for Barbarians was a clear anti-Nazi story detailing the impact of Nazi occupation, but from the perspective of children. It even featured scenes of children given homework to solve problems on bombing and of how to arrest Jews. The story concludes with one of the children turning against his own father, a farmer, and turning him over to the Nazi occupiers for purposely refusing to provide extra grain to the soldiers. The other children are disturbed by this act of treachery and it 'causes revulsion among some of the boys, and the picture ends with a definite feeling that there is a growing spirit of revolution in the village against their Nazi masters'.[43]

School for Barbarians is not alone in the 38 PCA records in its anti-Nazi themes or of its warnings of the horrors of Nazi occupation. *Cry Havoc* presents an 'alternative history' as a means of alluding to the horrors of the Third Reich, with a story set in the 'mythical central European country, Austro-Serbania' and featuring a dictator called Heilbrun who commands 'green and brown-shirted troupers'.[44] But in contrast to *Cry Havoc*, which was seen to be unacceptable to the PCA due to its depictions of a character that was a clear allusion to Adolf Hitler, *School for Barbarians* was deemed acceptable under the provisions of the Production Code in September 1939. Almost a year later, however, in June 1940, Edward Small sought Joseph Breen's own personal opinion as to the suitability of the project, which Breen provided:

> While we [PCA] are of the opinion that the story, as we read it, is acceptable under the provisions of the Production Code, it is my *personal* opinion that you ought to procede [sic] with great care before deciding to put a story of this kind into production, now'.[45]

There is no archival documentation that provides an explanation as to why Small was seeking Breen's personal counsel on *School for Barbarians*, though Breen's above letter to Small does indicate one potential motivation. Breen commented that a cycle of anti-Nazi films had emerged in the past twelve months, many of which—according to reports received by Breen—were not performing well at the box office. As Breen saw it, *School for Barbarians*, if produced, would come at the end of this cycle and would leave Small '"holding the bag" with your picture, after the others have run their course'.[46] In other words, Small faced a commercial risk in producing *School for Barbarians*, as well as a reputational risk following an increasing political backlash against this cycle of films.

However, as well as considering the risks outlined above, Small may have been considering his own wider business interests and those producers with whom he was in competition. Included in the *School for Barbarians* file are three documents that are concerned with the contractual status of the project. The first is a letter from the offices of the law firm Mitchell, Silberberg, Roth & Knupp to Joseph Breen, dated June 1940. The letter explains that attached to it is an excerpt of the contract for the sale of the project's script to Edward Small, which details how Small could refuse to pay the writers should Breen withhold his approval. However, that had not happened. Instead, Small had to request Breen for his *personal* opinion. It seems that Small was using Breen's opinion as a means of suggesting that the script had not received approval, which was obviously not the case. As the above law firm made clear to Small,

> No matter what Mr. Breen's opinion of the business wisdom of the producing of a picture is, or the desirability of such a picture, he can only refuse his approval if the proposed script contravenes the Code. In this instance there seems to me to be no such contravention and it would seem that if an approval of the script is requested it must be forthcoming.[47]

The documentation seems to suggest that Small was looking for a contractual loophole, as the law firm itself realised:

> If after a perusal of the Code and the letter in question you feel that I have overlooked some factor in arriving at this view, or if you find the basis for another conclusion, I would deeply appreciate your telling me so and giving me the opportunity to pursue the matter further.[48]

Small followed up on the suggestion of trying to find a minor indiscretion in the script that might constitute a violation of the Production Code. He resubmitted the script to the PCA on June 28, 1940, for the sole purpose of finding out 'whether or not, upon further examination, there was anything in the script which might be in violation of the Code, and which would thus arrant its rejection by us'.[49] Unfortunately, the PCA could not find any grounds on which to reject the script, despite what they called Small's 'efforts on his part to secure from us a rejection of this story'.[50]

With no further archival documentation, it is not possible to tell from the PCA records alone what Small's motivations were in ensuring *School for Barbarians* remained unmade. Intriguingly, Small's actions are not anomalous in the 38 PCA records: the producers of *Cry Havoc* also sought a rejection from the PCA in order for that project to remain unmade. In a letter to Joseph Breen, the producer James Townsend revealed his production company's motivations:

> I want you to know how much I appreciate your very fine letter regarding Charles Bennett's story 'CRY HAVOC!' Your comments are so right and will prove most helpful in our efforts to dispose of the story and I hope that someday I will be able, in my small way, to return your most generous gesture. Naturally, I am keeping your comments as confidential and personal to me.[51]

There was a twisted logic at work with both *School for Barbarians* and *Cry Havoc*, with the producers themselves responsible for the projects remaining unmade. This could have been because the respective projects were dealing with politically sensitive topics: Nazi Germany, a looming war in Europe, anti-Semitism, and so on. Both films were anti-Nazi productions and had more than likely originated at a point long before the outbreak of war in Europe was guaranteed. Yet, by the time the projects had reached the preproduction stage, global circumstances had changed. As such, the producers were looking for ways out of what had become controversial and politically sensitive pictures.

*

While projects like *Spy Ships* or *Cry Havoc* came up against political sensitivities and vested interests related to World War Two, others like *The Inquest*, *Civil Rights Story*, and *Child Labour* encountered challenges from domestic political forces that were in opposition to any representations that challenged the existing social and capitalist economic system of the USA. *Child Labour* was a particular case in point. The file for this project is incredibly sparse, made up of just three documents totalling fifteen pages: two letters and one story outline. Of the two letters, one is a standard submission letter from Columbia Pictures to the PCA, dated February 1937, while the other is a response letter from Joseph Breen, in which he outright rejects the project:

> I regret to be compelled to advise you that the material, in its present form, is quite definitely not acceptable under the provisions of the Production Code and is likewise suggestive of enormous difficulty at the hands of political censor boards, both in this country and in Europe [...] Our earnest recommendation to you is that you dismiss this present treatment from any further consideration.[52]

The PCA's verdict was unequivocal: not only was *Child Labour* not suitable for production, but no subsequent revisions would make it so. Fundamentally, the story was viewed as being 'subversive of the common weal'.[53] So just what had led the PCA to such a forthright judgement?

An original story written by Guy Endore and Martin Berkeley, *Child Labour* is, at its heart, a social problem film concerned with poverty and, quite obviously as the title implies, child labour. Endore and Berkeley prefaced the story outline submitted to the PCA with their own motivations, placing the story within the wider political contexts of the administration of President Franklin D. Roosevelt and his New Deal of the 1930s: 'The subject of child labour assumed importance not only because it is the greatest evil still permitted to flourish in American life, but also because it is certainly doomed to extinction within the term of the present administration'.[54] Interestingly, the preface of this unmade film in itself suggests that it was born out of an idea for another unmade film, reflecting the exploratory process of creative writing. The authors note that the idea for *Child Labour* stemmed from a story they had been writing based on the true life of Benjamin Harrison Rodd, a wealthy lawyer and politician who was appalled by the conditions in small-town America. Upon writing *Child Labour*, 'of the original Benjamin Harrison Rodd idea, nothing remains but the name of the leading character'.[55]

Child Labour centres on Rodd, a lawyer and candidate for the State Legislature, who visits the home of a local textile manufacturer, James

Rollins. Rodd's campaign is sponsored by Rollins who, in return, wants Rodd to vote against a forthcoming bill outlawing child labour. During his visit to Rollins' home, Rodd falls in love with the manufacturer's daughter, Diana. But it his tour of the textile factory that leaves Rodd disturbed, shocked by the working conditions of the children there. His mind becomes filled with 'the numerous children of the courtyard—their underfed bodies, their hopeless little faces. He had always known of child labor, of course, but a mill filled with as many kids as a schoolhouse is new to him'.[56]

As Rodd's relationship with Diana grows, he confides to her of his anger and disgust at the treatment of the children at her father's factory. Diana defends her father, arguing that the children are from a 'backward section of the hills who are being given a great opportunity by her father'.[57] The pair's conversation becomes heated and Diana accuses Rodd of being a 'pocket statesmen' for her father, and therefore a hypocrite: 'You know you'll jump when my father says jump—otherwise you won't be elected!'[58] Diana's accusation infuriates Rodd, who proclaims that the election does not matter to him and that he does not need her father's financial support or cultural network.

Rodd becomes acquainted with one of the children from the factory, Joe. He visits him at his home, a poor neighbourhood. Together, they devise a plan to bring about the downfall of Rollins and his factory: Joe will lead all of the children in a sit-in, locking themselves in the factory. Meanwhile, Rodd secures the support of the children's parents. Rollins attempts to retaliate against this shutdown of his factory by calling in the local police. By utilising the 'resistance' of the parents, Rodd drives the police away: 'The town is in uproar. Rodd is in a real fight and having the time of his life'.[59]

To aid the children in their sit-in, Rodd arranges food parcels. In response, Rollins orders that water and gas supplies to the factory be shut off. It is interesting to note that these sections of the outline have been annotated, presumably by administrators at the PCA. Whoever read the outline underlined sentences that highlight fighting or revolutionary action, or worse the death of any of the children. One such sentence—'her father is trying to starve the kids out'—has thick red pen heavily scrawled underneath it, bringing attention to the word 'starve'. Rollins demands that the National Guard be called in by the state's governor in order to bring about the end of the strike, but 'the governor refuses to go down in history as a modern Nero and turns Rollins down cold'.[60] When some of the children do die of starvation, it causes public outrage, forcing Rollins to back down and agree to arbitration. The strike leads to the opposition of the child labour amendment being dropped, which enrages Rollins:

> Rollins turns on Rodd, 'You've been very clever, Mr. Rodd, but you've outsmarted yourself. If I have to employ adult labour, my competitor will undersell me and I'll be forced to close the factory…then there will be no work for anyone.' Rodd Grins, 'I was expecting that, Mr. Rollins. But if you withdraw your opposition to the Child Labour Amendment, your competitors will be compelled to hire grownups too.'[61]

Child Labour is a story with wider allusions to the corruption at the heart of US politics. In its depiction of the relationship between the business owner and the politician, it reveals an insight into the dynamics of political life in the USA and the way money influenced democracy. It is a radical story, one that exposes a truth about the USA (and other Western democracies) that is ugly. The tone of Breen's rejection letter indicated the shock he felt at reading *Child Labour* and the way it proposed revolutionary action in order to overthrow the accepted order of political and cultural life, calling it 'inflammatory'.[62]

In particular, *Child Labour* provides explicit details about the ways in which left-wing groups could frustrate capitalism. Take, for example, the way it depicts trade union politics, such as in the moment that the children's sit-in begins: 'Acting on Rodd's instructions, [Joe] calls the kids away from their machines and holds a meeting'.[63] The story even outlines the way in which workers could organise against their bosses: 'A round table discussion follows at which Joe and several others are there with Rodd to represent the kids. Joe presents the strikers' demands'.[64] And it suggests the means of resistance against capitalist forces:

> There were only two ways for him [Rodd] to get up in this world—string with Rollins or fight him. He is fighting him and playing for big stakes. If he can lick Rollins, the political machine, and the bosses, he is a made man.[65]

Child Labour presents the revolutionary struggle of Rodd and the children as a successful cause, vindicating their violent actions and with no punishment for those involved. This latter point caused particular concern for Breen, who said,

> The scenes, depicting public disorder, riots, mobs in violent conflict with the police, and other such demonstrations, are particularly

> questionable as screen material in this present day, with so much public disorder evident on all sides in our national life.[66]

Child Labour was, simply put, too dangerous for how it suggested working people could take control of the means of production and chase out of town the capitalist forces of America. It suggested wholesale revolution and the toppling of the accepted political order and, as such, it would remain unmade.

*

The political forces that contributed to the unmade in Hollywood were broad and often bureaucratic organisations—the US Navy and the CFAA, for example—that were unrelenting and unreasonable in demands for a project to be left unmade. The power of these organisations and the censorious pressure they placed on the PCA and producers was considerable, with no compromise being made as a favour to the producer in question. The case of *Navy Spy*'s rejection by a branch of the US Armed Forces demonstrates the structural political forces at work in the case of war films of the era, with the US government and its military and intelligence agencies sensitive to the geo-political situation prior to the outbreak of World War Two and the unknown and unintended consequences that Hollywood films might have. Similarly, trade industry associations were indicative of powerful business lobbies determined to ensure self-promotion and positive representation for their members. Associations such as the CFAA clearly had a high-powered cultural network that they could draw upon to enact pressure—'important people', as they are ominously termed in the *Circus Parade* file. These structural forces—forces that the PCA had no control over but which was just as much at the whim of as the producers—were intent on keeping a stable political order and preserving the economic, cultural, and social systems of the USA, however unequal.

Yet, the most intriguing aspect of the analysis of the 38 PCA records is the revelation of the self-destructive behaviour of producers themselves who perversely sought ways of ensuring their own projects remained unmade. *School for Barbarians* and *Cry Havoc* are two important case studies that indicate that unmade projects may result from the insular vested interests of a single producer seeking to protect their reputation, finances, or something else altogether. The process of self-sabotage by producers highlighted in this chapter is an area ripe for extensive scholarly investigation.

Notes

1 Letter from Jason Joy to Will Hays, January 20, 1932, *Congai*, PCA records, The Margaret Herrick Library Digital Collection (MHLDC).
2 Letter from Maurice McKenzie to Jason Joy, October 22, 1928, *Circus Parade*, PCA records, MHLDC.
3 Letter from Karl Kae Knecht to Will Hays, October 18, 1928, *Circus Parade*, PCA records, MHLDC.
4 Ibid.
5 Letter from Maurice McKenzie to Jason Joy, October 30, 1928, *Circus Parade*, PCA records, MHLDC.
6 Letter from Maurice McKenzie to Jason Joy, October 25, 1929, *Circus Parade*, PCA records, MHLDC.
7 Letter from Maurice McKenzie to Jason Joy, October 14, 1929, *Circus Parade*, PCA records, MHLDC.
8 Letter from Julia Kelly to Jason Joy, October 21, 1929, *Circus Parade*, PCA records, MHLDC.
9 Letter from Jason Joy to Maurice McKenzie, October 28, 1929, *Circus Parade*, PCA records, MHLDC.
10 Letter from Maurice McKenzie to Jason Joy, October 30, 1929, *Circus Parade*, PCA records, MHLDC.
11 Letter from Frank Wilstach to Jason Joy, November 1, 1929, *Circus Parade*, PCA records, MHLDC.
12 Resume, November 2, 1929, *Circus Parade*, PCA records, MHLDC.
13 Letter from Jason Joy to Frank Wilstach, November 4, 1929, *Circus Parade*, PCA records, MHLDC.
14 Letter from Jason Joy to Frank Wilstach, November 19, 1929, *Circus Parade*, PCA records, MHLDC.
15 Letter from Melvin Hildreth to Will Hays, November 20, 1929, *Circus Parade*, PCA records, MHLDC.
16 Letter from Frank Wilstach to Jason Joy, November 21, 1929, *Circus Parade*, PCA records, MHLDC.
17 Hildreth to Hays, November 20, 1929.
18 Letter from Frank Wilstach to Jason Joy, December 6, 1929, *Circus Parade*, PCA records, MHLDC.
19 Wilstach to Hildreth, November 21, 1929.
20 Letter from Frank Wilstach to Jason Joy, December 2, 1929, *Circus Parade*, PCA records, MHLDC.
21 Wilstach to Joy, December 6, 1929.
22 Letter from Frank Wilstach to H. L. Bogue, December 6, 1929, *Circus Parade*, PCA records, MHLDC.
23 Letter from H. L. Bogue to Wilstach, n.d., *Circus Parade*, PCA records, MHLDC.
24 Ibid.
25 Letter from Frank Wilstach to Jason Joy, December 9, 1929, *Circus Parade*, PCA records, MHLDC.
26 Ibid.
27 Ibid.
28 Letter from Wilford Deming, Jr. to Joseph Breen, January 28, 1938, *Spy Ships*, PCA records, MHLDC.

29 Letter from Joseph Breen to Wilford Deming, Jr., February 2, 1938, *Spy Ships*, PCA records, MHLDC.
30 Letter from Harry Sherman to Douglas McKinnon, February 3, 1938, *Spy Ships*, PCA records, MHLDC.
31 Reader's Report, 'Navy Spy', February 3, 1938, *Spy Ships*, PCA records, MHLDC.
32 Letter from Joseph Breen to Harry Sherman, February 4, 1938, *Spy Ships*, PCA records, MHLDC.
33 Letter from Irene Muto to Joseph Breen, February 15, 1938, *Spy Ships*, PCA records, MHLDC.
34 Ibid.
35 Ibid.
36 Letter from Wilford Deming, Jr., to the US Navy Motion Picture Board, February 24, 1938, *Spy Ships*, PCA records, MHLDC.
37 Ibid.
38 Letter from Rear Admiral R. S. Holmes to Wilford Deming, Jr., March 1, 1938, *Spy Ships*, PCA records, MHLDC.
39 Letter from Wilford Deming, Jr. to Rear Admiral R. S. Holmes, n.d., *Spy Ships*, PCA records, MHLDC.
40 Letter from Joseph Breen to Franklin Warner, July 7, 1938, *Spy Ships*, PCA records, MHLDC.
41 Letter from Edward Small to Joseph Breen, August 31, 1939, *School for Barbarians*, PCA records, MHLDC.
42 'School for Barbarians' Reader's Report, n.d., *School for Barbarians*, PCA records, MHLDC.
43 Ibid.
44 'Cry Havoc!' outline, October 26, 1938, *Cry Havoc*, PCA records, MHLDC.
45 Letter from Joseph Breen to Edward Small, June 22, 1940, *School for Barbarians*, PCA records, MHLDC.
46 Ibid.
47 Letter from Mitchell, Silberberg, Roth & Knupp to Louis Swarts, June 26, 1940, *School for Barbarians*, PCA records, MHLDC.
48 Ibid.
49 Memo for the Files, Re: 'School for Barbarians', July 8, 1940, *School for Barbarians*, PCA records, MHLDC.
50 Ibid.
51 Letter from James Townsend to Joseph Breen, November 7, 1938, *Cry Havoc*, PCA records, MHLDC.
52 Letter from Joseph Breen to Harry Cohn, February 26, 1937, *Child Labour*, PCA records, MHLDC.
53 Ibid.
54 'Child Labour', original story outline, February 24, 1937, *Child Labour*, PCA records, MHLDC.
55 Ibid.
56 Ibid.
57 Ibid.
58 Ibid.
59 Ibid.
60 Ibid.
61 Ibid.

62 Breen to Cohn, February 26, 1937.
63 'Child Labour', original story outline.
64 Ibid.
65 Ibid.
66 Breen to Cohn, February 26, 1937.

Works cited

Yogerst, Chris. 2020. *Hollywood Hates Hitler! Jew-Baiting, Anti-Nazism, and the Senate Investigation into Warmongering in Motion Pictures.* Jackson: The University of Mississippi Press.

7 Crime

The analysis in this chapter is of those unmade projects in which the representation of crime or criminals was a contributing factor to why they remained unmade. Whether it's the (at that time) crime of homosexuality, as in the case of *Civil Rights Story*, the crime of illegal immigration, as in the case of *The Exiles*, the portrayal of child criminals, as in *Seen but Not Heard*, the outrageous portrayal of convicted felons, as in *The Cecil Wright Story*, or the depiction of religious criminals, as in the case of *Joan of Arc*, the focus is on the cultural conditions of production and the forces that prevented these acts of crimes being creatively expressed.

Criminality also extended to the sensitivity of producing films in a global context, with international diplomacy and relations posing problems for a number of the projects across the 38 Production Code Administration (PCA) records. Projects such as *The Forty Days of Musa Dagh*, *Congai*, *Pancho Villa*, *The Crimson Jester*, *The Torrid Zone*, and of course *School for Barbarians* and *Cry Havoc* all faced problems in the depiction and representation of particular locales and nations, whether Nazi Germany or violent depictions of Mexican outlaws. The latter in particular is a concern of this chapter. I want to begin by considering the creative debris of unmade Mexican-set westerns and the attempts to prevent a cycle of films that portrayed the Mexican nation as endemically violent and criminal (Delpar 1984).

*

Of the 38 PCA records six are, in sum, about Mexico: *The Torrid Zone*, *Pancho Villa*, *The Crimson Jester*, *Santa Fe Uprising*, *Here Comes Pancho Villa*, and *Gun Glory*. These projects range in time period, with one cluster emerging between 1931 and 1938 and a second cluster emerging between 1946 and 1953. Typically, the projects can be framed in

DOI: 10.4324/9781003206118-7

some way as westerns, adopting as they do the iconography of that genre—guns, desert locales, shoot-outs—and taking place during the later nineteenth or early twentieth century. Two of the projects deal explicitly with the real-life revolutionary Mexican general and outlaw Pancho Villa and his associated gang.

To understand why Pancho Villa recurs as a character in the PCA's records of the unmade, I want to first consider the Mexican western *Here Comes Pancho Villa*, a project that emerged in 1931. The project was instigated by B. P. Schulberg, David O. Selznick, and Joseph von Sternberg at Paramount Pictures. It was to be an adaptation of Louis Stevens' *Here Comes Pancho Villa: The Anecdotal History of a Genial Killer* (1930), written for the screen by von Sternberg and Richard H. Diggs, Jr. The development of the project depended on the advice of the Mexican government. After the Hays' office received a copy of the novel from Paramount, Jason Joy liaised with Mexican officials about their reaction to its depiction of Pancho Villa. The sensitivity of the situation was clear on all sides, as demonstrated in a letter sent by Diggs to the MPDAA:

> As Mr von Sternberg said the other day, he is willing to throw the sympathy either toward or away from Villa, whichever the censorship requirements demand. May I have your opinion as to what changes will be advisable in order to make this story acceptable from the Mexican point of view.[1]

At the bottom of this letter, Diggs has scrawled in blue pen that the Stevens' book was 'all that we have to go on [...] We will not start work on a treatment until we have your advice that the story will not get us into difficulty'.[2]

We can begin to understand the difficulties to which Diggs was referring via a synopsis of Stevens' book that he sent to the MPDAA. The story focuses on Pancho Villa, an absolute degenerate described as 'Neroic', who wants to bed Violet, the wife of Fred Merril. Villa purchases concubines and sleeps with whomever he wants, but Violet is proving elusive, despite the fact that she is 'willing to flirt quite shamelessly with all the attractive men in the court'.[3] Her behaviour leads Villa to teach Merril a lesson and open his eyes to Violet's infidelity. Villa orders one of his own men to run away with Violet in the hope that Merril will pursue her. Villa then seeks to punish both Merril and Violet and orders them to be killed by a firing squad. However, the cartridges used turn out to be blanks: it is a prank designed to humiliate Merril. Merril escapes with his life, but leaves without his wife.

The synopsis, totalling four pages, appears incomplete and is focused on Chapters 15 and 16 of Stevens' novel. It also presents a particularly sadistic portrait of Villa and his Mexican gang, with the entire tone of the story being quite vicious and cruel, particularly in its depiction of women. In order to overcome any such negative portrayal of Mexico, Jason Joy arranged for von Sternberg to visit Mexican officials in Mexico City to ensure that the 'story may be authentic and inoffensive to the Mexican people'.[4] The reason for the overly cautious approach to *Here Comes Pancho Villa* stemmed from the growing tension between Hollywood and the Mexican government, with the latter believing that there was a persistent anti-Mexican theme in Hollywood-produced films, which constantly framed Mexicans as criminals.

The dynamics of the diplomatic situation were explained in a letter from Fred Herron, the Motion Picture Producers and Distributors of America's (MPPDA's) foreign manager, to Joy. The letter was received in early March, though not with any reference to *Here Comes Pancho Villa*. It instead discussed the wider ongoing problems of a production company called First National. The company was producing 'another picture' with Mexican villains in it, *Woman Hungry*. Herron was anxious about First National's approach to portraying Mexicans as criminals, stating that the company was 'getting away with murder on their Mexican stuff [...] but they are going to get into trouble sooner or later'.[5] Herron believed that First National was unnecessarily resorting to using 'Mexican types' as criminals in its films, when the company could just have easily used 'ordinary Western low class types of individuals'.[6] In using stereotypes of Mexicans as criminals, and seemingly getting away with it—not without causing considerable political trouble for the MPPDA—Herron felt it was encouraging other production companies and studios to follow suit, initiating a trend for representing Mexicans as criminals. As a result, the Mexican government was placing pressure on Herron to prevent these kinds of films and in turn Herron was now applying pressure on Joy. His reasons for doing so were clear:

> One of these days something is going to irritate the Mexican people anti-American wise, and the company that stands in the way of a flag waving piece of propaganda is going to get badly burnt [...] The slightest spark touches these people off down there in the wrong way and we are perfectly helpless when the flame is kindled, all we can do is to keep out of the way of the spreading fire and allow it to burn itself out. In the meantime, however, the whole industry suffers as well as the individual company.[7]

Amidst this political turmoil, the archival evidence indicates that Joy and the MPPDA seemed to be under the impression that *Here Comes Pancho Villa* could be used as a project to repair the damage inflicted on Hollywood's relationship with Mexico. Von Sternberg, despatched to Mexico City, was in effect being used as a diplomatic envoy on behalf of Hollywood. As Joy explained it to Herron,

> Von Sternberg will absorb so much atmosphere and good will that [*Here Comes Pancho Villa*] will turn out to be not only safe, but will contain so much favourable Mexican material that it will undo a lot of the damage that a lot of other pictures have caused.[8]

The *Here Comes Pancho Villa* file is unfortunately quite sparse, with available archival documentation not providing any indication as to the outcome of von Sternberg's trip. The file concludes with a series of notes from Jason Joy, in which he details how the two chapters from Stevens' book that Paramount was most interested in adapting were sent for approval to the Mexican Foreign Office. The final note is about a meeting that took place between Will Hays and Mexico's Secretary of Foreign Affairs, Senor Estrada, at which it was agreed that Hays would personally contact Estrada on all questions involving Mexico.[9]

The *Pancho Villa* file is for an unmade project from a year later, 1932, and was once again a planned adaptation of the life of Pancho Villa, this time being produced by David O. Selznick and Edward Montague at RKO Studios. The company had received an unpublished biography, *Pancho Villa*, from author Frank Fouce. RKO believed it had an advantage in any film produced about the life of Pancho Villa because Fouce himself was Mexican and was 'very close to Mexican politics, and what is more important close to what Mexicans like and dislike. He assures us that he can make this subject acceptable to the Mexican government'.[10] Attached to RKO's submission was a document titled 'Brief History of Francisco Villa', a factual account of the life and times of Villa. The one-page biography details Villa's brutality and crimes during the Mexican revolution that broke out in 1910, concluding how he had 'caused the death of several thousand during a period of ten years'.[11] Despite his violent history, the biography ultimately portrays Villa as a working-class hero:

> He became the leader of a band of highwaymen and for ten years was known to operate in the states of Chihauhau and Durango. He was well known for his daring and feared by the rich landowners

> and mining companies, but at the same time he became a hero to the poor for his many good deeds.[12]

RKO intended to set its story in 1915, when Villa had taken over Mexico City, supported by his outlaw army of over 40,000 men. After this initial success, Villa later suffered incredible losses, eventually retreating from Mexico City and his army rapidly decreasing in size. RKO's proposed story also focused on Villa's raid on Columbus, New Mexico, which provoked the American government into pursuing him for over a year.

Accompanying the 'Brief History of Francisco Villa' is a document titled 'Recommendations on the Pancho Villa Film'. The document lists suggestions on how to placate the Mexican government and to avoid any negative representations of the Mexican nation as inherently criminal and violent. This included the need for a heavy emphasis on Villa having no official government role, instead stressing how he had 'split with the government due to his personal ambitions' and that he was 'aided by other malcontent rebel chiefs'.[13] The list of recommendations is insightful for the way it was steering the producers of the *Pancho Villa* project away from criminal stereotypes, including the need to:

- Avoid vulgarity and disrespect for women by the Mexican characters.
- Avoid filthy sets or scenery portraying Mexico.
- Avoid ridiculing of the habits, looks, and clothing of the Mexican characters in general.
- Portray Villa's good or bad deeds as individual characteristics of an unusual man, rather than typical characteristics of his race.
- Avoid all scenes which will reflect against the Mexican people.[14]

The recommendations were necessary in order to ensure that any proposed film of the life of Pancho Villa met with the approval of the Mexican government.[15] However, the Mexican government would only approve an actual script, not an outline or treatment. This meant that RKO had to be prepared to risk the financial investment in a project that more than likely would face opposition from the Mexican government. Unfortunately, other circumstances beyond anyone's control curtailed the planned production: Edward Montague, the film's primary producer, died unexpectedly in September 1932. Prior to his death, Montague had discussed the difficulty in producing a film about the life of Pancho Villa with Selznick, concluding that no amount of reassurance given to the Mexican government or any subsequent approval of the script would guarantee a film could be successfully produced. One way of mitigating the financial risk was to ask a writer to produce a script on the basis of a fee deferral, thereby avoiding any potential loss.[16] With Montague having died, it was up to Selznick to decide whether the risk was worth it. Yet, there is no archival evidence in the *Pancho Villa* file of Selznick's decision, with the final document being a letter from Selznick to Joy that simply read: 'Thank you for your note on the Pancho Villa matter'.[17]

Still, it is possible to get a sense of the structural barriers that Mexican westerns faced across the full spectrum of the six Mexican-themed projects in the PCA records and understand how, in each case, the Mexican government was largely responsible for the projects remaining unmade. The creative debris and fragments of correspondence left behind are all reflective of the frustration caused by the diplomatic tension between Hollywood and Mexico in the 1930s to 1950s. The *Santa Fe Uprising* file, for example, shows how the independent producer, Ben Pivar, had his script—which was deemed acceptable under the provisions of the Production Code—sent to an external Latin American adviser, Addison Durland. The reason for involving Durland was because *Santa Fe Uprising*'s principal criminal and his gang were all Mexicans.

The *Santa Fe Uprising* file does not reveal why the project was abandoned, but it does provide an insight into the approach being taken within the industry to Mexican-set films. Durland wrote up a three-page letter that assessed the offensiveness of *Santa Fe Uprising*, a film that he determined was incredibly problematic because it dealt explicitly with the Mexican American War of 1846–1848. Durland noted how many projects that were about the war, either directly or indirectly, had previously been left unmade due to political sensitivities: 'Mexico lost almost half of its national territory [...] Just to show how dangerous the matter was considered, even references to the siege and slaughter at the Alamo were eliminated'.[18] Durland was worried about the prospect of the Mexican American War featuring in *Santa Fe Uprising*, mainly because Ben Pivar's company, Reliance Pictures, was an independent company not affiliated to any major studio. This, Durland felt, meant Pivar was less likely to be dissuaded from producing the film:

> The reason why Mr. Ben Pivar is going to produce this picture is because he has obtained a good deal of footage from some film

> made years ago by Small, 'Kit Carson', I believe it was called. At any rate, he has gone so far as to have a shooting script ready and to ask him to eliminate dangerous episode and characters would really be asking him to shelve the story which he will not and cannot do unless willing to suffer a considerable loss of money invested so far.[19]

Pivar faced considerable financial risk in producing a picture that would more than likely remain unmade as a result of ongoing political tensions that had their origins in the very war he was trying to depict on screen. Durland, while feeling empathy for Pivar's situation, sensed he would become a 'test case' for the industry more broadly:

> The question is one more of Pan American policy than anything else, that in spite of all his efforts to deal with the delicate subject fairly and properly [*Santa Fe Uprising*] still might be considered offensive by Mexico, and that in such a case many complications might arise which might harm him and the entire industry.[20]

The situation facing producers of Mexican-themed westerns or war films depended entirely on the level of criminal depiction present in the story. Therefore, if a story dealt explicitly with the life of a well-known bandit, such as Pancho Villa or, in the case of *The Crimson Jester*, Emiliano Zapata, the chances are it was bound to remain unmade, unless there was considerable distancing of the character from an association with Mexico. The archival documentation shows how the PCA would defer to the judgement of either external advisers on the Latin American situation or, more fatal for the producer and planned project, Mexican government officials.

Still, producers found stories of such criminal folk heroes alluring. *The Crimson Jester*, in its depiction of the life of Emiliano Zapata, is part of a cluster of criminal films in the 38 PCA records, along with the likes of *The Cecil Wright Story*, dealing with criminal biography. The producers of *The Crimson Jester*, Walter Wanger and Charles Boyer, had no hope of being able to bring the film to the screen. It was a planned adaptation of the book of the same name by H. H. Dunn. Submitted to the PCA in April 1938, the book was described as being about the culture of Zapata and his hordes of men, which numbered 20,000 and 'most of whom were pure-blooded Mexican Indians. The story has to do with this marauding and riotous living, and is marked by what is probably the most amazing story of butchery and looting which has ever been written'.[21] As Fred Herron summarised it, the book was little more than the true story of 'murder, rape, robbery, and everything else done in the manner of the Huns of ancient Europe'.[22]

The Crimson Jester was a project that faced challenges to its production on two fronts: one, from Mexican authorities due to its depiction of a Mexican outlaw and, two, the PCA for its breach of the provisions of the Production Code in relation to brutality, violence, and gruesomeness. These two challenges were linked, as the PCA itself argued:

> If anything like an accurate biographical story were to be made, from the life of Zapata, it would be almost impossible to tell the story, without suggesting the grossest kind of brutality. On this score alone, the material is enormously dangerous.[23]

The PCA was only passing judgement on the novel, as no treatment had been submitted by Wanger, but on the basis of the book alone the PCA could not perceive how any element of it could be successfully adapted for the screen. As a result, Wanger decided not to pursue the project.[24]

The aspect of *The Crimson Jester* that seemed to cause most concern for the PCA was its romantic depiction of Zapata and his outlaws. The criminals of the story were being framed as sympathetic—anti-heroes—and Zapata himself as 'a romantic character, carefree, a gay dog, fearless, dashing and brave'.[25] It was a problem that several of the unmade projects in the 38 PCA records faced, with a lack of appropriate justice being meted out against those who committed criminal acts. Too often, producers were letting their fictional criminals get away—quite literally—with murder. The sympathetic portrayal of criminals—and to some extent the villainous portrayal of the justice system—was certainly the reason for another project in the PCA records, *The Cecil Wright Story*, remaining unmade.

*

The Cecil Wright Story was a depiction of the real-life criminal Cecil Wright, a gangster that operated in the states of Illinois and Indiana in 1930 and committed a series of burglaries, holdups, and automobile thefts. The script for *The Cecil Wright Story* was sent to the PCA in April 1950 by producer Sam Baerwitz of Belsam Productions.[26] The PCA notified Baerwitz that it could not provide an opinion on the script in the first instance because the story largely focused on Cecil Wright's incarceration at the Leavenworth and Alcatraz prisons.

Instead, the PCA had to defer to the judgement of the United States Department of Justice's Bureau of Prisons. As Breen explained,

> There is a provision under the Production Code which states, 'the history, institutions, prominent people and citizenry of all nations shall be represented fairly'. [...] it is mandatory upon us to make certain that those two institutions [Leavenworth and Alcatraz] and the personnel there are properly presented.[27]

The automatic involvement of an external organisation beyond the PCA typically, in the case studies analysed, proved to be fatal for a project. Inviting other stakeholders into the approval process meant dealing with forces that were primarily concerned with their own organisational reputation and perception management, not with the production of motion pictures. The Bureau of Prisons was not going to be easy on *The Cecil Wright Story* and Breen probably already knew this. After all, the script was a true story about the life of a career criminal and, unless the film portrayed Cecil Wright in exactly the way he had been convicted by the Department of Justice, there was little hope that the project would succeed. Breen's letter to Baerwitz amounted to a death knell for *The Cecil Wright Story*, but a protracted process of attempting to convince external government forces of the merit of the story ensued.

It was the Director of the Bureau of Prisons, James V. Bennett, that provided a verdict on *The Cecil Wright Story*, and he saw a fundamental, almost philosophical problem at the heart of the story's logic, summed up by the statement at the start of the script: 'a true story'. The story suggested that Cecil Wright was a victim of the justice system:

> I appreciate that the motion picture code relates only to insuring a fair portrayal of American institutions. But 'institution' is a broad term and may well be construed to include not only courts, prosecuting offices and penal establishments as such, but also our entire American judicial system. On this theory I would think there is ample basis for condemning the entire script as a gross misrepresentation of the facts.[28]

The Cecil Wright Story file is made up of 37 individual documents, of which 30 are some form of correspondence. There is no creative material. Instead, it is possible to reconstruct the story from the correspondence between the Bureau of Prisons and the producer, Sam

Baerwitz. In doing so, what is revealed is not so much the intricate plot details of the script, but the opposing cultural and political outlooks of these two stakeholders and the way they were clashing over the philosophical question of how truth and reality should be represented on screen, or what even constitutes truth and reality. Baerwitz's argument was based on the script being an imagined reality: this was a film, nothing more. For Bennett, the script was perpetuating a lie about a real-life figure, which would impact on the public perception of American justice. Bennett even said that the script, if produced, would play a 'gigantic hoax on the American motion picture public'.[29] Bennett was objecting to the script's depiction of the federal prison system in the USA and also its wrongful depiction of Cecil Wright:

> If this play is filmed and displayed before the public, it will constitute a grave disservice to the cause of public respect for the processes of law, our courts, and our penal institutions. Cecil Wright in this screenplay is depicted as a hero of triumph over the courts. He is a man who simply did nothing wrong and was a victim of legal indifferences and injustice.[30]

The battle over the truth of Cecil Wright's conviction led to a series of exchanges between Bennett and Baerwitz to prove who was right, with Bennett even sending affidavits that were used in the conviction of Wright to back up his own argument. Bennett also outlined in detail, in a letter to Baerwitz, the history of Cecil Wright as he saw it. Bennett refuted the script's suggestion that Wright was transferred from Leavenworth to Alcatraz because he had set up a law 'office' in his cell and was providing legal advice to fellow inmates. Instead, Bennett argued that in 1941 Wright was transferred to Alcatraz for agitating and causing a prisoner's strike. Bennett also refuted a scene in which Wright saved the life of a prison officer during the transfer to Alcatraz, with the officer having drunk too much alcohol. According to Bennett, this never happened, calling it 'pure fiction'.[31] Bennett objected to the portrayal of the prison officers at Alcatraz and the explicit naming of real-life officers. The script also depicted a riot that took place at the prison while Wright was incarcerated there, but with Wright portrayed as a hero of the affair, which, according to Bennett, 'he was not'.[32] Bennett also rejected the scenes of Wright's actual conviction, which he said misrepresented the trial.

All of Bennett's points came back to the issue of the script being a 'true story'. He felt that, if the film was produced as a fictional story, he'd have had less grounds on which to object against it.[33] But as he saw it, if the film was to be produced as a true story, then it had to be brought in line with what he called 'the actual facts and the record. [...] he is not dealing with a fictional story but with a true-life story involving actual persons and agencies responsible for the administration of Federal justice'.[34]

In contrast, as Baerwitz saw it, the script was truthful, informed as it was by his collaboration with the former Assistant Attorney General of California, William O'Connor, who had helped Wright win his freedom. The script was based on O'Connor's own story of Cecil Wright's conviction and incarceration.[35] Baerwitz revised the script in the hope of overcoming the Bureau of Prisons' objection, but to little avail. Bennett, by January 1951, still opposed Baerwitz's alternative history of Wright, one that contradicted the official history contained in the files of the Department of Justice. As a compromise, the PCA recommended that Baerwitz delete the foreword to the script that proclaimed it a 'true story', that he change the name of the main character from Cecil Wright to a fictional name, that the action of the story be moved from Illinois to other parts of the USA, and that it be set in prisons other than Leavenworth and Alcatraz.[36] In other words, the PCA was telling Baerwitz to produce an entirely different film, something which Baerwitz could not accept.

The correspondence continued into the spring of 1951, with Baerwitz making further changes, though none of them substantive. He even seemed to enhance the forward to the script, which was submitted to the PCA on June 15, 1951, as part of a document titled 'The Cecil Wright Story Changes':

> This is a true story. Cecil L. Wright is the living proof that we are almost the only nation on earth where no matter how low the flame of justice may dip, it never goes out. Cecil L. Wright believed. He believed that at the end there would be those men and those courts who would protect and cherish his birthright, his heritage as an American. After spending nearly 18 years in several prisons, he still says: 'I AM NOT BITTER—I DON'T HATE ANYONE'.[37]

Baerwitz, along with the screenwriter he had hired, Stephen Longstreet, was emphasising how the story was about the purported miscarriage of justice, which Bennett simply did not agree with. As long as Baerwitz continued along this path of placing his version of the truth at the centre of *The Cecil Wright Story*, it was bound to remain unmade. The Bureau of Prisons refused to compromise until appropriate revisions were made. For Baerwitz, this caused considerable frustration, as he told the PCA in August 1951: 'Needless to tell you how I feel. I have spent a small fortune in acquiring the rights to this story'.[38] Baerwitz was placing his principles before profit and was paying the price. In the end, *The Cecil Wright Story* was depicting a truth that the Department of Justice just did not want audiences to see and as a result remained unmade.

*

Throughout *The Cecil Wright Story* file, there are repeated examples of someone within the PCA annotating correspondence, with a particular focus on sentences that highlighted how criminals were being portrayed sympathetically. This is because, under the provisions of the Production Code, 'crimes against the law shall never be presented in such a way as to throw *sympathy with the crime, as against law and justice, or to inspire others with a desire for imitation*'.[39] This did not just apply to films that depicted violent criminals, whether Mexican outlaws or mid-western gangsters, but also congenial figures too. Take the example of *The Exiles*, a proposed story about a German academic that flees Nazi Germany using a fake passport. While he was a respectful figure, and his motivations were understandable, the PCA objected to the main character escaping justice for his violation of immigration law, with the audience

> led to feel sympathy with someone that has broken immigration laws, which is serious violation of code. [...] If these actions caused resentment among that section of the public which looks with disfavour upon the migration here of anybody from abroad, while domestic unemployment is so great, then this would be further aggravated.[40]

Even if a character guilty of a crime killed themselves, a story was still deemed as lacking a compensating moral outcome, i.e. justice. In the case of *Payment Delayed*, in which the main character is guilty of murder, the PCA objected to the main character's suicide as it meant they defeated the 'due processes of law'.[41]

In those instances where the PCA was the barrier to a film about or containing crime being produced, there was an element of contradiction, particularly when the subject of crime intersected with sex. Take the example of *Civil Rights Story*, a project that was being developed by MGM in 1950. The story was about a newspaper editor in southern USA who was waging a war against a local gang of racketeers (the gang was involved in gambling and prostitution rings, as well as drug trafficking) by publishing stories of their activities:

> The newspaper man is a highly respected citizen of the town, happily married, with 2 children, and quite successful. He apparently leads a life which is completely irreproachable. The racketeers however uncover the fact that the editor is a homosexual. The editor is confronted with a choice of either stopping his campaign or being exposed.[42]

The newspaper man, despite knowing full well that his homosexuality will be revealed, decides to involve the Department of Justice, and ensure that the racketeers are convicted. His sacrifice forces him to leave his home, his family, and his job and to seek a new identity in a new town. Despite the fact that the story explicitly brought to justice criminals, the PCA was much more concerned with the depiction of homosexuality and could not approve *Civil Rights Story* 'so long as it had anything whatever to do with homosexuality, prostitution, or the drug traffic'.[43] Instead, the PCA proposed an alternative situation, in which the man was not gay, but rather that his wife was schizophrenic and confined to a mental hospital, and it was this that the racketeers used to bribe him. The PCA felt that this substantive change would allow the story to become one in which the newspaper man was forced to choose between serving society and exposing the racketeers or endangering his wife.

While the suggested change to *Civil Rights Story* is of course problematic—and there is no archival evidence in the file that details whether the changes were made or not—it is reflective of the cultural conditions of the era. Still, it does also indicate the level of contradiction and indeed the hypocrisy when it came to films about crime. When it came to films that portrayed crime, stakeholders at the PCA and elsewhere were more concerned with the management of perception and reality: how did a film represent criminals and who, as a result, was seen as being the true villain? The Department of Justice? An entire population? Or the PCA? Crime was acceptable on screen, but only insomuch as it did not damage the reputation of established institutions and governments. Otherwise, these organisations would coalesce to ensure a project remained forever unmade.

Notes

1 Letter from Richard Diggs, Jr., to Association of Motion Picture Producers, February 26, 1931, *Here Comes Pancho Villa*, PCA records, The Margaret Herrick Library Digital Collection (MHLDC).

2 Ibid.
3 'Here Comes Pancho Villa', synopsis, February 26, 1931, *Here Comes Pancho Villa*, PCA records, MHLDC.
4 Col. Joy's Resume, March 11, 1931, *Here Comes Pancho Villa*, PCA records, MHLDC.
5 Letter from Fred Herron to Jason Joy, March 13, 1931, *Here Comes Pancho Villa*, PCA records, MHLDC.
6 Ibid.
7 Ibid.
8 Letter from Jason Joy to Fred Herron, March 18, 1931, *Here Comes Pancho Villa*, PCA records, MHLDC.
9 Col. Joy's Resume, December 14, 1931, *Here Comes Pancho Villa*, PCA records, MHLDC.
10 Letter from Edward Montague to Jason Joy, August 9, 1932, *Pancho Villa*, PCA records, MHLDC.
11 'Brief History of Francisco Villa', n.d. *Pancho Villa*, PCA records, MHLDC.
12 Ibid.
13 'Recommendations for Pancho Villa Film', n.d. *Pancho Villa*, PCA records, MHLDC.
14 Ibid.
15 Memo, 'Pancho Villa', August 23, 1932, *Pancho Villa*, PCA records, MHLDC.
16 Letter from Jason Joy to David O. Selznick, September 16, 1932, *Pancho Villa*, PCA records, MHLDC.
17 Letter from David O. Selznick to Jason Joy, September 19, 1932, *Pancho Villa*, PCA records, MHLDC.
18 Letter from Addison Durland to John McCarthy, December 8, 1947, *Santa Fe Uprising*, PCA records, MHLDC.
19 Ibid.
20 Ibid.
21 Memo for the Files, Re: 'The Crimson Jester (Zapata of Mexico)', April 15, 1938, *The Crimson Jester*, PCA records, MHLDC.
22 Letter from Fred Herron to Joseph Breen, April 14, 1938, *The Crimson Jester*, PCA records, MHLDC.
23 'The Crimson Jester (Zapata of Mexico)', April 15, 1938.
24 Letter from Walter Wanger to Joseph Breen, April 16, 1938, *The Crimson Jester*, PCA records, MHLDC.
25 'The Crimson Jester (Zapata of Mexico)', April 15, 1938.
26 Letter from Sam Baerwitz to Joseph Breen, April 4, 1950, *The Cecil Wright Story*, PCA records, MHLDC.
27 Letter from Joseph Breen to Sam Baerwitz, April 13, 1950, *The Cecil Wright Story*, PCA records, MHLDC.
28 'Cecil Wright Story—Proposed Screen Play', May 3, 1950, *The Cecil Wright Story*, PCA records, MHLDC.
29 Ibid.
30 Letter from James V. Bennett to Joseph Breen, May 4, 1950, *The Cecil Wright Story*, PCA records, MHLDC.
31 Letter from James V. Bennett to Sam Baerwitz, May 4, 1950, *The Cecil Wright Story*, PCA records, MHLDC.

32 Ibid.
33 'Cecil Wright Story—Proposed Screen Play', May 3, 1950.
34 Letter from James V. Bennett to Joseph Breen, May 4, 1950, *The Cecil Wright Story*, PCA records, MHLDC.
35 Memo for the Files, Re: 'The Cecil Wright Story', February 21, 1951, *The Cecil Wright Story*, PCA records, MHLDC.
36 Ibid.
37 'The Cecil Wright Story Changes', June 15, 1951, *The Cecil Wright Story*, PCA records, MHLDC.
38 Ibid.
39 Memo for the Files, Re: 'The Exiles', June 1938, *The Exiles*, PCA records, MHLDC.
40 Ibid.
41 Letter from Joseph Breen to Jack Jungmeyer, March 12, 1946, *Payment Delayed*, PCA records, MHLDC.
42 Re: 'The Exiles', June 1938.
43 Ibid.

Works cited

Delpar, Helen. 1984. 'Goodbye to the "Greaser": Mexico, the MPPDA, and Derogatory Films, 1922–1926'. *Journal of Popular Film and Television* 12, no. 1: 34–41.

8 Conclusion

So what is to be gained from this analysis of the 38 designated 'unproduced' Production Code Administration (PCA) records? On one level, it is about focusing attention on their existence within the archive and about amplifying the category of the unmade, unseen, and unreleased within other archives around the world. On another level, it is about making clear the materiality of film history. The unmade, unseen, and unreleased is explicitly linked to its existence in the archive. In looking at the 38 PCA records one thing is certain: there are many gaps and absences, with abrupt halts in documentation and the history being conveyed. I have purposely avoided consulting any material outside of this sample in order to emphasise its material dimensions and to circumvent attempts at resolving these frustration and absences, bringing to the fore the fact that there are gaps in empirical evidence and gaps in existing knowledge and gaps in history. That is the entire purpose of archival research and unproduction studies.

The analysis of the 38 PCA records also raises various questions and topics for consideration in the future development of unproduction studies. Most obvious of all is how there is a need to instigate a process of detective work to uncover more of this kind of material. This book is just the start of a much wider archival mapping exercise. Undoubtedly, while some of the unmade projects in the PCA records have no other existing material available in any other repository, others may have related material in other archives. Just because the archival evidence trail comes to a dead end in this particular archival collection does not necessarily mean that there is no other evidence available somewhere else in the world. Unproduction studies scholars just need to find it. That will take a lot of work because many of the individuals discussed in this book are marginalised, forgotten, and overlooked with no dedicated archive of their own. Further archival evidence

DOI: 10.4324/9781003206118-8

relating to, say, Edna Riley, probably does exist, but it is about extensive digging to find out where. Maybe in the archives of studios like Twentieth Century-Fox or Paramount, or maybe even in a random archive somewhere else in the USA. And the material more than likely is hidden, off-catalogue, perhaps remaining uncatalogued. The work to locate the unmade, unseen, and unreleased requires a global research effort, one that will involve a collaboration between academics and archivists. It is a major endeavour to say the least.

The analysis has also shown how, despite the lack of creative material for a variety of factors at times, non-creative archival documentation that is available can be far more revealing than creative material. Whether it is interoffice memos that betray particular cultural attitudes, or the annotations on correspondence that make it clear the kinds of issues that really concerned particular individuals or organisations, these documents can evidence motivation, ideas, and outcomes. While undoubtedly a romantic concept, unproduction studies is not just about 'lost' projects or screenplays. Instead, for unproduction studies scholars, there are greater stakes and much more to understand beyond the actual script. That is not to dismiss substantial creative material. Far from it, given how I emphasised the importance of recreating the unmade through innovative public engagement activities in Chapter 1. Rather, this case study has tried to underscore how even the most trivial of archival documents can tell us more than we actually thought possible.

There is also the issue of how archives of the unmade reveal an entire industrial system predicated on investing finances, resources, and labour into projects that will never be produced, and with no intention of ever producing them. The American film industry has, over the course of its existence, developed a system based primarily on unproduction, with the vast majority of projects destined to always remain in a cycle of development, abandonment, potential resurrection, and then archivisation. Those projects that break through into the cycle of production, post-production, distribution, and exhibition are rare. Archives of the unmade reveal the extent of how this system of unproduction financially sustains not only screenwriters, but an array of other administrative workers, including lawyers, accountants, secretaries, and beyond, all working—quite often knowingly—on projects of the unmade (Fenwick, forthcoming). They are a hidden labour force within history because their object of work remains hidden and absent from history. The industrial logic of Hollywood—of how it works—is not one based on the produced, but one based on the unmade.

However, I think the most important outcome of this analysis of the 38 PCA records is how the archival documents show that the reasons for a project remaining unmade during the Production Code era was quite often not the fault of the PCA, at least in the case of the analysed sample. There were many other forces at work and what is apparent is how the forces are much more nuanced than expected. Business interest. Self-destruction. International diplomacy. Capitalist forces. Patriarchal forces. Indeed, the debris and fragments that remain of the unmade are indicative of the encounters of producers and screenwriters with these structural barriers, often revealing conflicts of ideology and culture, and emphasising how all creativity is inherently political. The archival fragments of Edna Riley's *All Flags Flying* are the material evidence of such encounters and conflicts. They are the traces of the patriarchal society being perpetuated and of endemic misogyny and sexism across the industry. Similarly, the archival documents of a number of other unmade projects are evidence of how men were complicit in perpetuating a discourse of sex and women as a danger to society and in ensuring that Hollywood output furthered the hegemony of the patriarchy. Similarly, those projects that attempted to tell stories of revolution or expose the hypocrisy of big business and politicians were thwarted by a range of often hidden interests that sabotaged any threats to the existing world order. The unmade is symptomatic of the hegemony of capitalism and American dominance in an increasingly globalised world. All of these unmade films are from a time when Hollywood was taking over the world and was one of the key image brands of the USA. Any material that was subversive of America's capitalist system was just not compatible. Yet, whether these same structural forces persist in contributing to the unmade in contemporary Hollywood is a deeper question that requires further research.

Perhaps this last point is the real outcome of this book. There is an abundance of archival material available for unproduction studies to make sense of and to help construct this shadow history of the unmade, a history that counters the story of privilege which dominates in current histories of Hollywood. This is a project that will take many years, decades even, with the scale of the challenge overwhelming. But the shadow history of the unmade that I am proposing exists is about a systematic study of all available archival evidence, locating it, analysing it, and contributing it to a wider unproduction studies project. One-off case studies will not achieve this goal, nor one-off monographs. This book shines only a pinpoint of light into the vast darkness of that shadow, hidden, and overlooked history. It is a long-term research effort, which in itself indicates the viability and longevity of unproduction studies and the study of the unmade, unseen, and unreleased.

Work cited

Fenwick, James. forthcoming. 'John Boorman's *The Lord of the Rings*: A Case Study of an Unmade Film.' *Historical Journal of Film Radio and Television*.

Appendix I

Unproduced files in the PCA records

PCA Record Title	*Time Period Covered by the Records According to Metadata*	*Production Company/ Producer According to Catalogue Metadata*	*Production Company/Producer Named in Archive Documents*	*Genre*
All Flags Flying	1934–1935	Paramount	• 20th Century Fox (1934) • Paramount (1934)	• War • Romance
Burning Secret	1934–1964	None Specified	• Universal (1934) • Warner Bros. (1936) • 20th Century Fox (1947) • Harris-Kubrick Pictures Corporation (1956) • MGM (1956; 1964)	• Crime • Romance
Case History	1950–1953	Columbia	• Columbia (1950–1951) • Jerry Wald (1950–1953)	• Crime
Child Bride	1938 (the record actually contains material from 1943 to 1948, with nothing dated 1938)	Columbia (incredibly misleading)	• Columbia (sent a memo about the genre in 1938) • Raymond Friedgen (1943) • Astor Pictures (1943) • Mr. Kunody (1948)	• Romance • Social problem drama • Exploitation
Child Labor	1937	Columbia	• Columbia (1937)	• Social problem drama

(*Continued*)

PCA Record Title	*Time Period Covered by the Records According to Metadata*	*Production Company/ Producer According to Catalogue Metadata*	*Production Company/Producer Named in Archive Documents*	*Genre*
Circus Parade	1928–1929	James Cruze	• Sono-Art (1929) • James Cruze (1929)	• Crime
Civil Rights Story	1950	MGM	• Nicky Nayfack (1950) • MGM (1950)	• Crime
Congai	1929–1938 (material from as early as 1926)	MGM	• Sam Harris (1929) • Pathe (1929) • Universal (1929–1930) • Carl Laemmle Jr. (1930) • Hunt Stromberg (1938) • MGM (1938) • Lamar Trotti (1930–1931) • Irving Thalberg (1932) • Paramount (1931–1932) • Charlie Sullivan (1932) • RKO (1930; 1932) • Ben Schulberg (1932)	• Romance • War
Coquette	1936–1947	None specified	• Pioneer Pictures (1936–1937) • Merian Cooper • RKO (1937) • MGM (1938; 1946–1947)	• Crime • Romance
Cry Havoc	1938	Charles Bennett	• Myron Selznick and Co (1938) • Charles Bennett (1938)	• Spy thriller

Gun Glory	1946–1953	MGM	• MGM (1946) • Columbia (1948) • MGM (1952–1953) • Robert Vogel (1952) • Dore Schary (1952–1953)	• Western
Here Comes Pancho Villa	1931	None specified	• Paramount (1931) • Schulberg (1931) • Von Sternberg (1931) • Selznick (1931) • Lasky (1931)	• Western
High School Wives	1945–1946	Alex-Stern	• Alexander Stern Productions (1945) • Jack Schwarz Productions (1946)	• Social problem drama
House of Mist	1946–1948	Paramount	• Hal Wallis Productions (1946–1948) • Paramount (1946–1948)	• Romance
Joan of Arc	1933–1943	None specified	• RKO (1933–1934) • M. G. Whitman (1933–1934) • Val Lewton (1936) • Selznick International (1936; 1943) • Hal Wallis (1936) • Sam Katz (1938) • MGM (1938)	• Religious epic
Love by Force	1954	Goldstone	• Goldstone (1954) • Universal (1954)	• Romance

(*Continued*)

PCA Record Title	*Time Period Covered by the Records According to Metadata*	*Production Company/ Producer According to Catalogue Metadata*	*Production Company/Producer Named in Archive Documents*	*Genre*
Love Child	1932–1936	Columbia	• Jack Cohn (1932) • Columbia (1932; 1934; 1936) • Harry Cohn (1934; 1936)	• Romance
Lysistrata	1930–1940	Morros	• Harry Ginsberg (1934 • Hal Roach Studios (1934 • MGM (1930; 1934) • Boris Morros Productions (1940)	• Ancient Greek comedy
Pancho Villa	1932	None specified	• RKO (1932) • Edward Montague (1932) • David Selznick (1932—contacted because Montague dies)	• Western
Payment Delayed	1946	None specified	• PRC (1946) • Imperial Productions (1946) • Universal (1946)	• Murder mystery
Santa Fe Uprising	1947	Small	• Ben Pivar (1947) • Reliance (1947) • Edward Small Productions (1947) Are the top two contracted to Small? Pivar's/Reliance correspondence is on a small letterhead	• Western
School for Barbarians	1939–1940	Small	• Edward Small (1939–1940)	• War
Seen But Not Heard	1936	Paramount	• Paramount (1936) • RKO (1936)	• Crime drama

Ships in the River	1946	Warner Bros.	• Warner Bros. (1946) • Charles Hoffman (1946)	• Crime • Social problem drama • Romance
Spy Ships	1938	Fine Arts	• General Pictures Corp (1938) • Wilford Deming Jr. (1938) • Franklin Warner (Fine Arts Studio) (1938) • Harry Sherman Productions (1938)	• Spy thriller
The Cecil Wright Story	1948–1951	Belsam	• Belsam Productions (1950–1951) • Sam Baerwitz (1950–1951)	• Crime
The Crimson Jester	1938	Walter Wanger Productions	• Walter Wanger Productions (1938)	• Western • Crime
The Exiles	1938–1941	Goldwyn	• Sam Goldwyn (1938)	• Political thriller • Drama
The Forty Days of Musa Dagh	1934–1964	MGM	• MGM (1934–1935; 1938–1939; 1950; 1964) • David O' Selznick (1934; 1936) • Irving Thalberg (1935) • Rouben Mamoulian (1950) • Robert Vogel (1964)	• Historical epic • War
The Inquest	1950	Film Group	• Film Group (1950) • Forrest E. Judd (1950)	• Romance
The Torrid Zone	1936	RKO	• RKO (1936)	• Romance • Political thriller
The Vicious Circle (largely referred to in the documents as *Bitter Fruit*)	1946–1947	Wilder	• Oswald Productions (1946) • Richard Oswald (1946) • Monogram (1946) • Gabriel Pascal (1947) • Samuel Goldwyn Studios (1947) • W Lee Wilder Productions (1947)	• Social problem drama

(*Continued*)

PCA Record Title	*Time Period Covered by the Records According to Metadata*	*Production Company/ Producer According to Catalogue Metadata*	*Production Company/Producer Named in Archive Documents*	*Genre*
The Weather in the Streets	1936–1937	Selznick	• Carl Laemmle Jr. (1936) • Selznick International Pictures (1937) • Val Lewton (1937)	• Romance
There's One in Every Town	1951	20th Century Fox	• David Hempstead (1951) • 20th Century Fox (1951) • Philip A. Waxman Productions (1951)	• Crime drama
Those Who Trespass	1950	Laurel Films	• Laurel Films (1950)	• Crime • Murder mystery
Two against Tomorrow	1939	Garnett	• Walter Wanger Studios (1939) • Tay Garnett (1939)	• Romance • War
Wanted for Murder	1945	PRC	• PRC (1945)	• Crime
White Gorilla	1944–1945	Supreme	• Supreme Pictures Corp (1944) • A. W. Hackel (1944)	• Exploitation • Action

Index

For Product Safety Concerns and Information please contact our EU representative GPSR@taylorandfrancis.com
Taylor & Francis Verlag GmbH, Kaufingerstraße 24, 80331 München, Germany

www.ingramcontent.com/pod-product-compliance
Lightning Source LLC
LaVergne TN
LVHW010950110826
845149LV00015B/3283

* 9 7 8 1 0 3 2 0 7 2 4 8 7 *